'Jennifer Guest's creative worksheets serve as reminders, a̲ ̲c̲r̲e̲a̲t̲i̲v̲e̲ ̲o̲p̲e̲n̲i̲n̲g̲s̲, ̲a̲s̲ "soothers" in the therapeutic journey. Self, couples and family in context invites clients and therapists to consider the inter-relational nature of our co-existence through evocative and provocative drawings and reflective questions. This is a gem indeed.'

– Imelda McCarthy PhD,
Fifth Province Centre, Dublin

'Few resources offer something that can be used tomorrow by both new and experienced therapists alike. I will be using these worksheets for two reasons. First, Guest provides a sound theoretical underpinning that belies their accessibility. Second the resources follow a pattern of exploration that build one upon the other as clients develop understanding of self and other.'

– Dr Rachel Davies, Chartered Counselling Psychologist
and Senior Practice Consultant at Relate

'This is a rich resource, full of excellent conversation starters or inner reflections. The sheets provide something really useful and tangible from ideas that can be difficult to articulate. This would be useful for family therapists (or others focused on relational work) to use within sessions to explore meaningful stories.'

– Alexandra Gill, Systemic Family Therapist

'A thoughtful, beautifully presented set of worksheets. Use of these will kick-start conversations and will add depth to therapeutic work by inviting clients of all ages to write, draw and explore. Children, adults and whole families will benefit from using these lovely relational tools.'

– Dr Sarah Helps, Consultant Clinical Psychologist, Systemic Psychotherapist,
Tavistock and Portman NHS Foundation Trust

'One might appreciate this workbook because of the variety of really useful invitations it makes to clients, to reflect on their lives. One might also appreciate it for its simply designed worksheets (which can be coloured-in). One might appreciate it for the many ideas it entertains and stimulates for clients and practitioners alike. I think you will find yourself in it and simply appreciate it by using it well.'

– Kieran Vivian-Byrne, The Family Institute, University of South Wales

THE ART ACTIVITY BOOK FOR RELATIONAL WORK

100 ILLUSTRATED THERAPEUTIC WORKSHEETS TO USE WITH INDIVIDUALS, COUPLES AND FAMILIES

Jennifer Guest

Jessica Kingsley *Publishers*
London and Philadelphia

First published in 2017
by Jessica Kingsley Publishers
73 Collier Street
London N1 9BE, UK
and
400 Market Street, Suite 400
Philadelphia, PA 19106, USA
www.jkp.com

Library of Congress Cataloging in Publication Data
Names: Guest, Jennifer, author.
Title: The art activity book for relational work : 100 illustrated therapeutic worksheets
to use with individuals, couples and families /Jennifer Guest.
Description: London ; Philadelphia : Jessica Kingsley Publishers, 2017. |
Includes bibliographical references.
Identifiers: LCCN 2016041521 | ISBN 9781785921605 (alk. paper)
Subjects: LCSH: –Handbooks, manuals, etc.–Handbooks, manuals, etc. |
Marital psychotherapy–Handbooks, manuals, etc. | Family
psychotherapy–Handbooks, manuals, etc.
Classification: LCC RC480.5 .G842 2017 | DDC 616.89/1562–dc23 LC
record available at https://lccn.loc.gov/2016041521

British Library Cataloguing in Publication Data
A CIP catalogue record for this book is available from the British Library

ISBN 978 1 78592 160 5
eISBN 978 1 78450 428 1

Printed and bound in the United States

For all of us, living together in this systemic world.

Acknowledgements

I would like to express many thanks to all my clients and colleagues, who, over the years, have helped bring these worksheets to life, especially those at Bradford Relate. Also, grateful appreciation to the theorists who have devoted their lives and careers to therapy and the infinite development of helping people to experience happier, healthier, more peaceful lives and relationships. I have given credit to individual theorists where I have knowingly designed a worksheet from their particular work, and there are many pages designed from techniques I've come across over the years which I'm unfortunately unable to give specific credit to: None of these have been created where the source of the credit is known and not mentioned. Thanks also to everyone involved at Jessica Kingsley Publishers, for their part in enabling this book to become available to so many.

Contents

Introduction

The worksheets in this book have been developed and designed from many years' therapeutic clinical practice with clients. Some of this work has been with individuals, some with couples and some with families. The content of the worksheets has been informed by the main themes and relational issues that people bring to the counselling room, along with key aspects from psychodynamic, narrative, cognitive behavioural and systemic theories. It's assumed that most clinicians will be familiar with the theoretical ideas mentioned in the chapters. They are included in order to provide the basic frameworks from which the worksheets have been developed.

Some worksheets ask specifically focused questions, while others aim to act as springboards for creative exploration, in which therapeutic change can arise. There are no instructions about how to use these pages, other than for clients to respond to the questions and tasks posed on the worksheets; they are open for interpretation in whatever way is most helpful. Their aim is to be an aesthetically-designed invitation for people to draw, paint or write their responses to these relational themes. Sometimes the worksheets may simply provide visual focus for issues being discussed. They can be valuable for work in the session, or for clients to complete at home. Having experienced how hugely beneficial it is to encourage clients in becoming creative about their problems and dilemmas, I wanted to combine this idea with the theoretical aspects, as described in the chapters.

People can find it helpful, soothing and mindful to doodle or colour in whilst thinking about difficult or painful experiences, and this can be incredibly cathartic. Each page gives an opportunity for people to do this whilst simultaneously focusing on the discussion points. The questions on the worksheets can simply be used as a visual prompt for people to start thinking about what the important issues are to them, to act as reminders for any 'homework' to be done in between sessions or as an outlet for producing creative works of art to do with their identity, relationships or ways of communicating.

The worksheets (which can be photocopied as well as downloaded from www.jkp.com/voucher using the code GUESTARTACT) have been divided up into the themes of the four chapters. There is much overlap, as many could be included in more than one chapter. The book isn't intended to be used from beginning to end, rather that specific pages are chosen by the client or practitioner as to what would be the most helpful and relevant. It's assumed that people using this book would be working within the safe arenas of therapy; if anyone chooses to use this book in isolation, please ensure that access to appropriate professional support is available, in case of any unexpected emotional responses to the themes presented here.

Chapter 1

Sense of Self

It's essential for our wellbeing that we have understanding about ourselves, in order to know what makes us feel happy, stimulated and motivated. It's also important information which impacts on how we develop meaningful relationships with others. People tend to begin this process of developing their identity in adolescence, some more consciously than others, and continue to do so throughout their adult lives. Part of this development is learning what our emotional needs are and how we express these to others.

Theoretical perspectives
Psychodynamic theory

Many of the worksheets in this chapter are aimed at helping people get to know themselves better. Some aim to identify emotional needs and to help people be proactive in defining who they want to be. This extends also to how they want to be in their relationships. Many of the pages focus on exploring our experiences from the past, including those from childhood, adolescence and previous relationships. The aim is to gain understanding of how these experiences have affected and shaped us.

The people around us are strong influences on the development of our sense of self, especially in our formative years throughout childhood. This is influenced by how we were related to by others, how much our needs were met and by whom. We absorb ideas of what a male, a female, a grandparent, a brother, a daughter, a teacher and so on is with an almost infinite list of roles. These ideas and understandings translate into meanings we attach in adulthood to the certain roles. In their book, *Family Therapy: 100 Key Points and Techniques*, this is described by Rivett and Street:

> Each person will be shown in their development certain ways of reacting to stress, being encouraged to relate to certain types of people and to have clear messages on how to produce and react to emotions. Each individual will be

presented, through his or her family history, with a blueprint of how a male or female life should unfold... The script will provide the framework on which a person will construct a self image... All family members are potentially able to experience the role of every generation: A woman in her later years may experience being a grandmother, a mother and a daughter...there is always a part of the self that is a forever a daughter and forever a mother... Try as we may we are unable to lose the experience childhood: the experience of being cared for in a certain way, of having certain behaviours expected of us and being given certain knowledge of ourselves and others. (2009, p.24)

Systemic theory

Few of us live in total isolation. There has been a shift in many arenas of psychotherapy to acknowledge the importance of significant people around us, in our families, our colleagues, in our communities, our cultures and the socio-political climates in which we live. Systemic theory uses this basis that a person is viewed *in the context* of how they live – that we are all parts of systems and subsystems – and this is hugely influential on how we behave and who we become (Bateson 1972). Rivett and Street write about viewing people as a part of the family system:

> From this perspective it is more accurate to describe individuals as communicating certain behaviours rather than describing them as a particular type of person... every behaviour is at one and the same time both an expression of that person and a communication to others... Individuals who live together and share intimate moments and tasks such as childcare, caring for the elderly, financial budgets, etc. have a continual stream of communication that contributes to the definition of who they are... Individuals are therefore part of the communication system we call the family and to be involved in a communication system continually is at the core of human identity... The cycle of interaction...becomes the focus and primary source of change...individuals are defined and maintained by circular interactional patterns of which they are a part. (2009, pp.9–14)

Narrative therapy

The focus here becomes what is socially constructed by our language alongside the context in which we live. Michael White and David Epston are prominent names in the development of these ideas. Writing about therapeutic conversations, White describes how people 'find themselves interested in novel understandings of the events of their lives...fascinated with neglected territories of their identities' (2007, p.5). Many worksheets in this chapter aim to be springboards for such conversations, providing a focus point for these explorations.

White and Epston termed the phrase 'externalisation' to describe the therapeutic benefit of placing someone's problem outside of the person and their identity, in order that the person gets clarity and new perspectives about how to deal with the problem. In *Maps of Narrative Practice*, White (2007, pp.24, 25) writes how a lot of those 'who seek therapy believe that the problems in their lives are a reflection of their own identity'. Also that their problems '...come to represent the "truth" of their identity'. Whilst being careful to stress that these conversational techniques are not about people disregarding responsibility for addressing their problems, he claims that new perspectives can be gained from creating a distance between a person's sense of self and the issues. He states, 'When the problem becomes an entity that is separate from the person...new options for taking action to address the predicaments of their lives become available' (2007, p.26).

Some of the worksheets in this chapter provide a focus point for people to explore these ideas about externalising problems, to inspire understanding for themselves and to help facilitate conversations about the ideas. White continues to describe this process:

> Externalising conversations...make it possible for people to unravel some of the negative conclusions they have usually reached about their identity under the influence of the problem... [They] have opened many possibilities for people to redefine their identities, to experience their lives anew, and to pursue what is precious to them... It is in the rich characterisation of problems that people's unique knowledges and skills become relevant and central to taking action to address their concerns. During this process, people become aware of the fact that they do possess a certain know-how that can be further developed and used to guide them in their effort to address their problems. (2007, pp.26, 43, 59)

The worksheets focusing on these externalisation ideas (the last 6 in this chapter) have been directly developed using the techniques described in White's work, to provide visual platforms for such conversations.

If emotional wellbeing is like a bank account...

+

0

—

Place positive experiences in this section, for e.g. love, support, achievements, hugs or compliments. >

These are deposits.

Negative experiences, such as traumatic events, unexpected losses, criticism or conflicts, are withdrawals.

Place these in this section. >

If our emotional wellbeing is 'in credit', it can be easier to cope with adverse and challenging events and experiences.

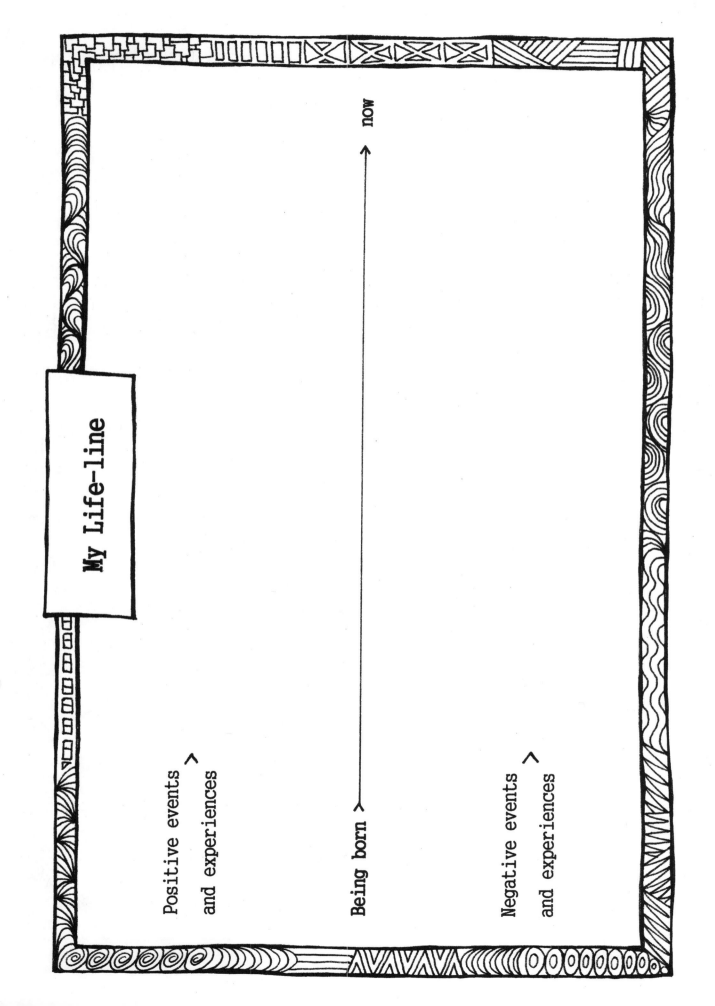

Reflecting back on your childhood, how much do you feel that your needs were met...

emotionally?

physically?

educationally?

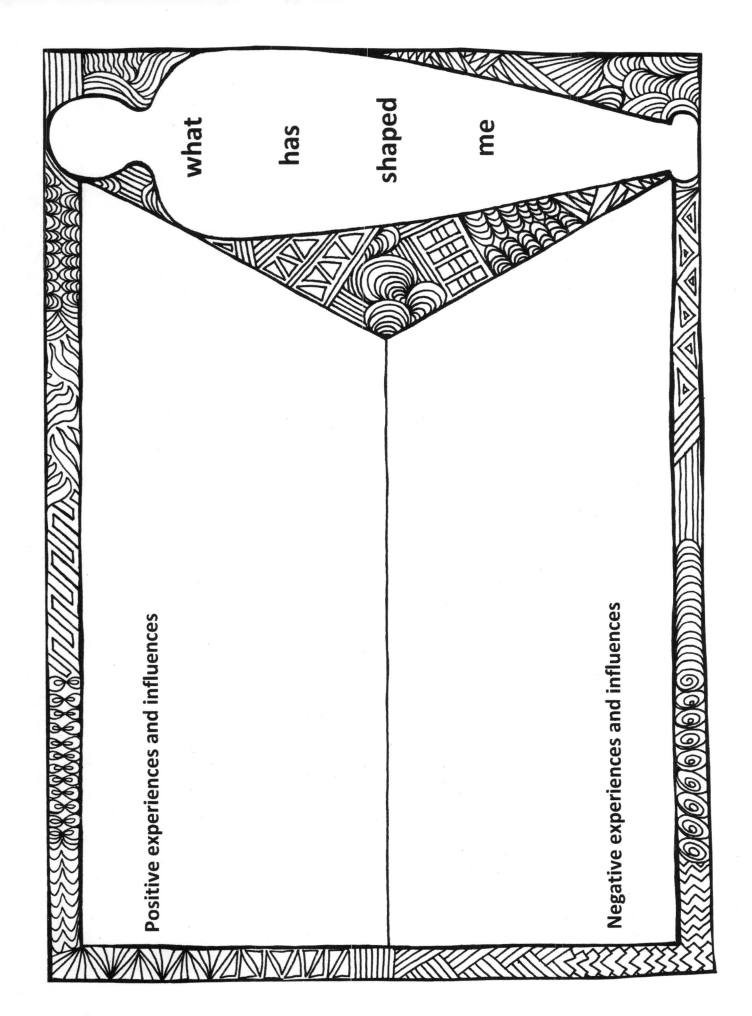

what has shaped me

Positive experiences and influences

Negative experiences and influences

Imagine putting your problems into a bag...

Which is the smallest, the biggest, the most urgent, the least distressing, etc.?

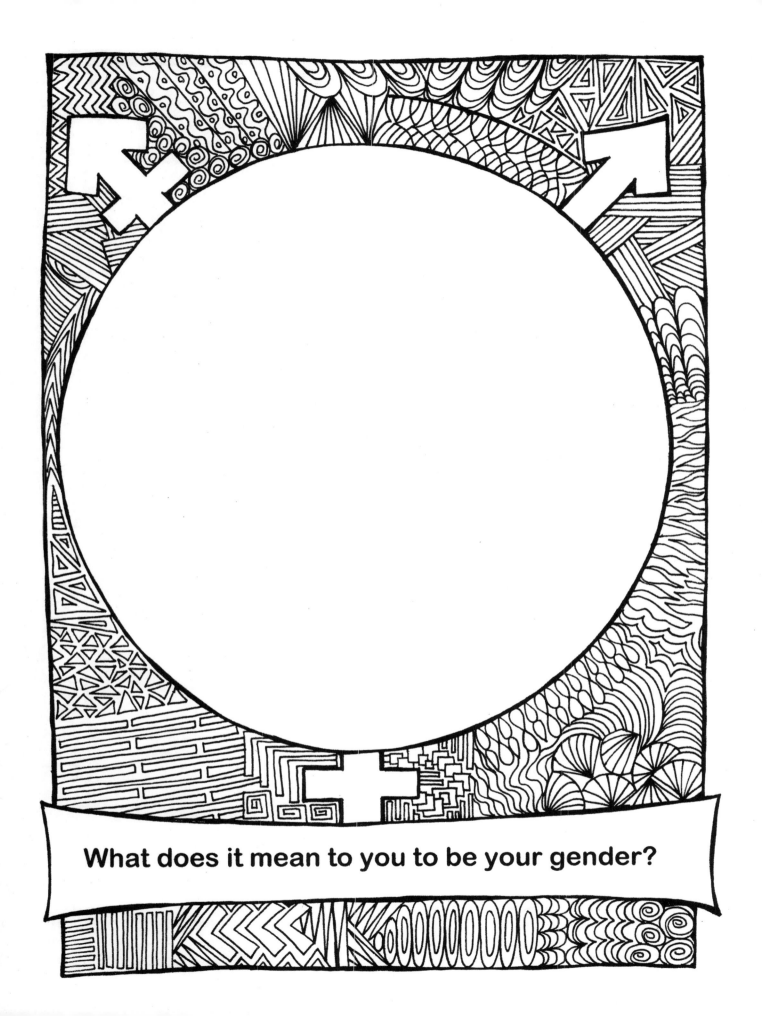

What does it mean to you to be your gender?

What's your experience of **making decisions...**

...throughout your childhood, at home and school?

...in previous relationships?

...in your work-life?

...currently?

For you to have **wellbeing**, what does this **mean to you?**

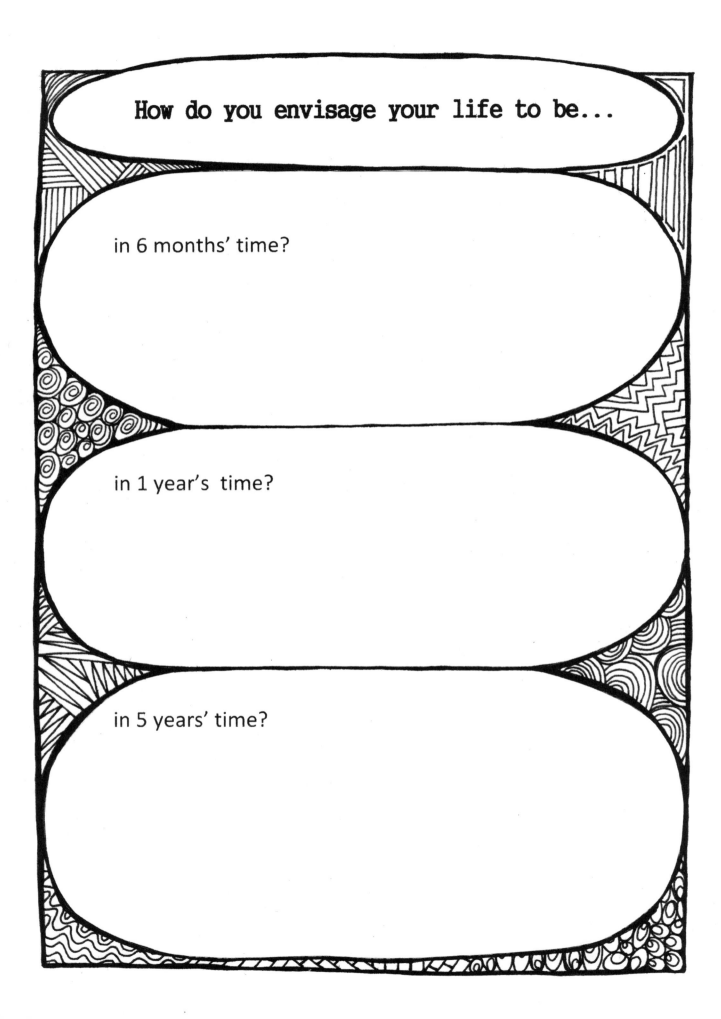

How do you envisage your life to be...

in 6 months' time?

in 1 year's time?

in 5 years' time?

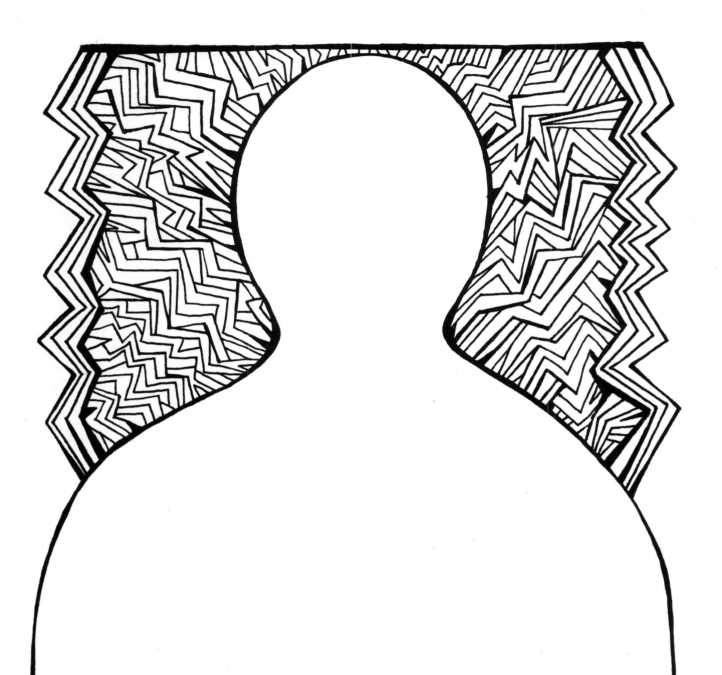

Hurt, disappointment, guilt, rejection or loneliness are often emotions going **on inside** when anger is being expressed on **the outside**.

Think back to the last few times you expressed anger: Were you feeling any **other emotions** internally?

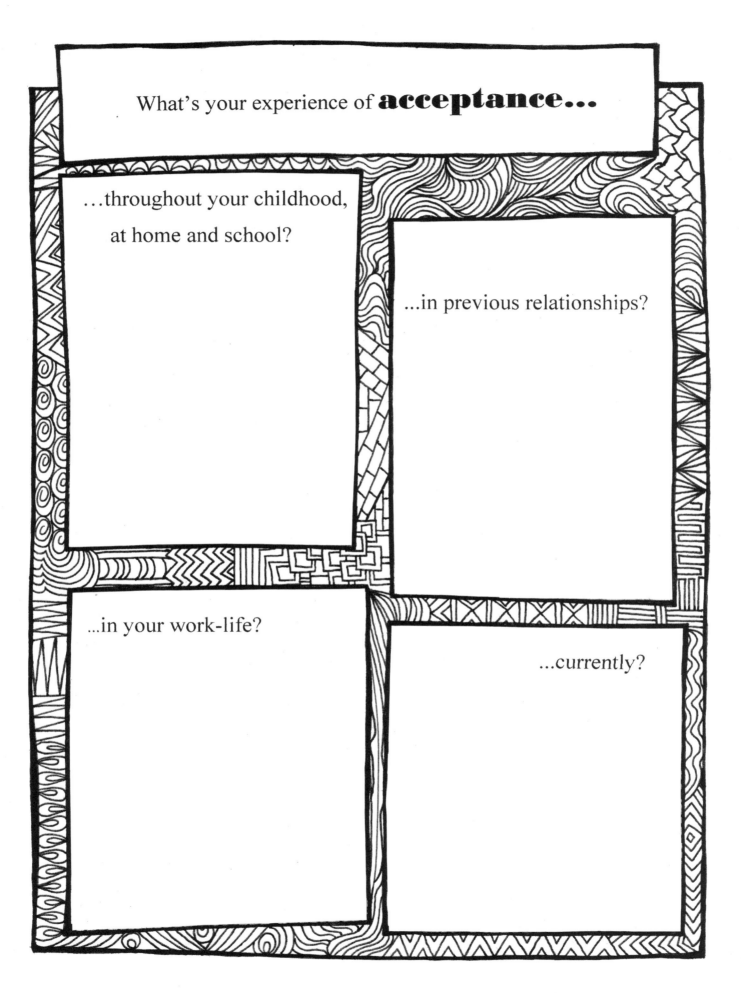

What's your experience of **acceptance...**

...throughout your childhood, at home and school?

...in previous relationships?

...in your work-life?

...currently?

What's the opposite of **acceptance?**

What's your relationship like with

acceptance

now?

What is your idea of a **man** in a relationship?

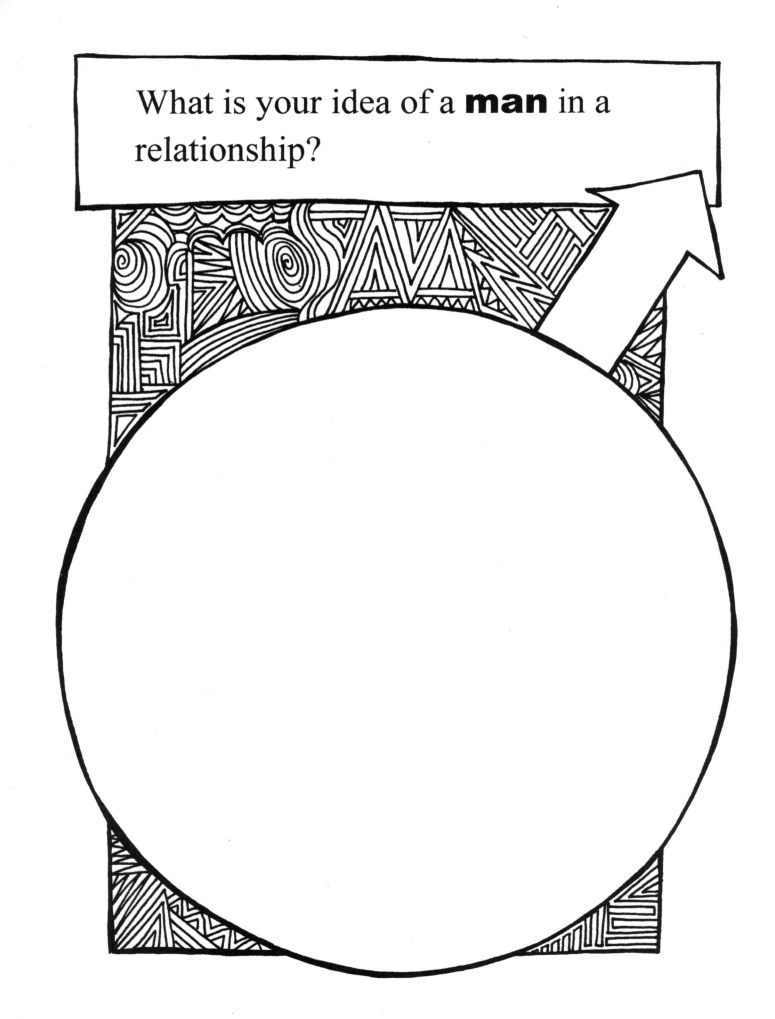

What is your idea of a **woman** in a relationship?

How would you describe
your **many selves**,
from the most
to the least
'**visible**'?

What **beliefs and values** are important to you around these aspects of life…?

Parenting

Careers

Finances

Household responsibilities

Future planning

Leisure time

Marriage/Partnerships

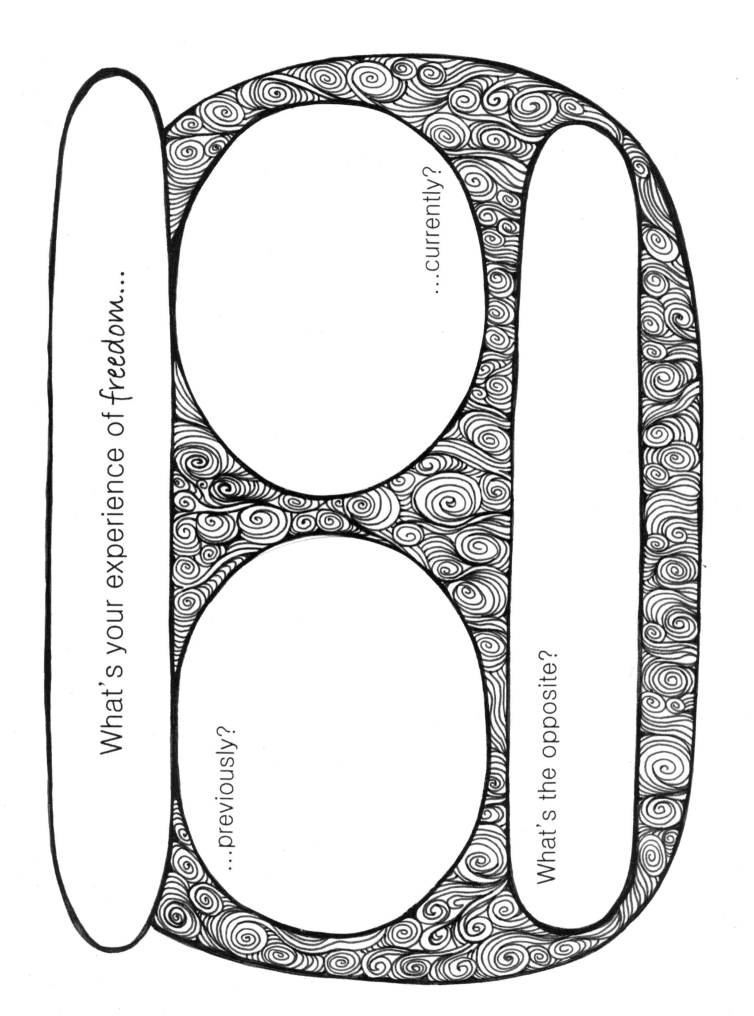

What's your experience of freedom...

...currently?

...previously?

What's the opposite?

What's your experience of **being or feeling alone**...

...currently?

...previously?

How is this different from, or similar to, feeling lonely?

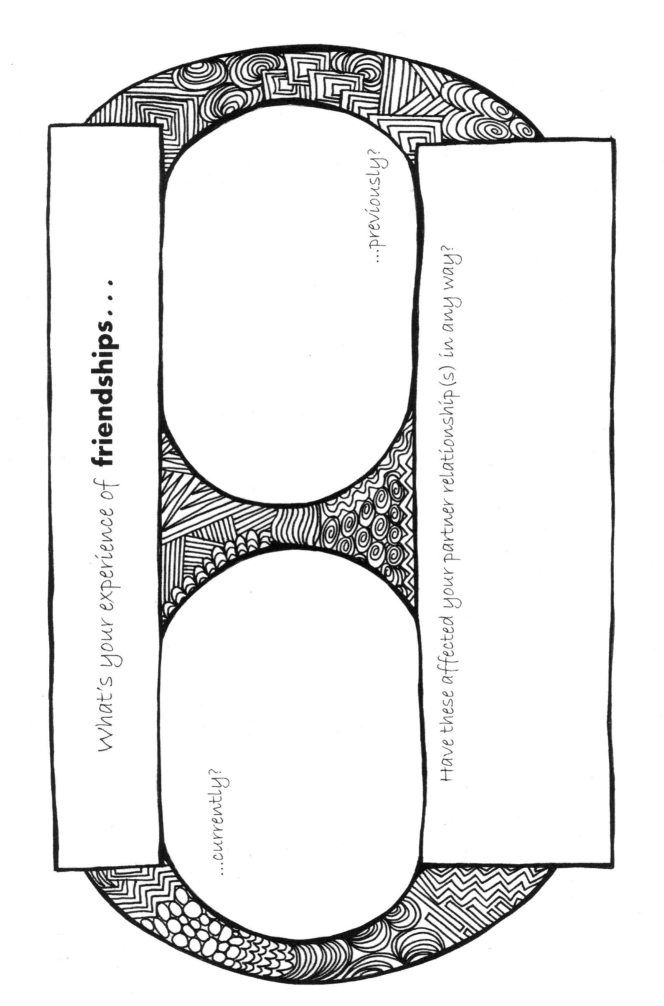

What's your experience of **friendships**...

...currently?

...previously?

Have these affected your partner relationship(s) in any way?

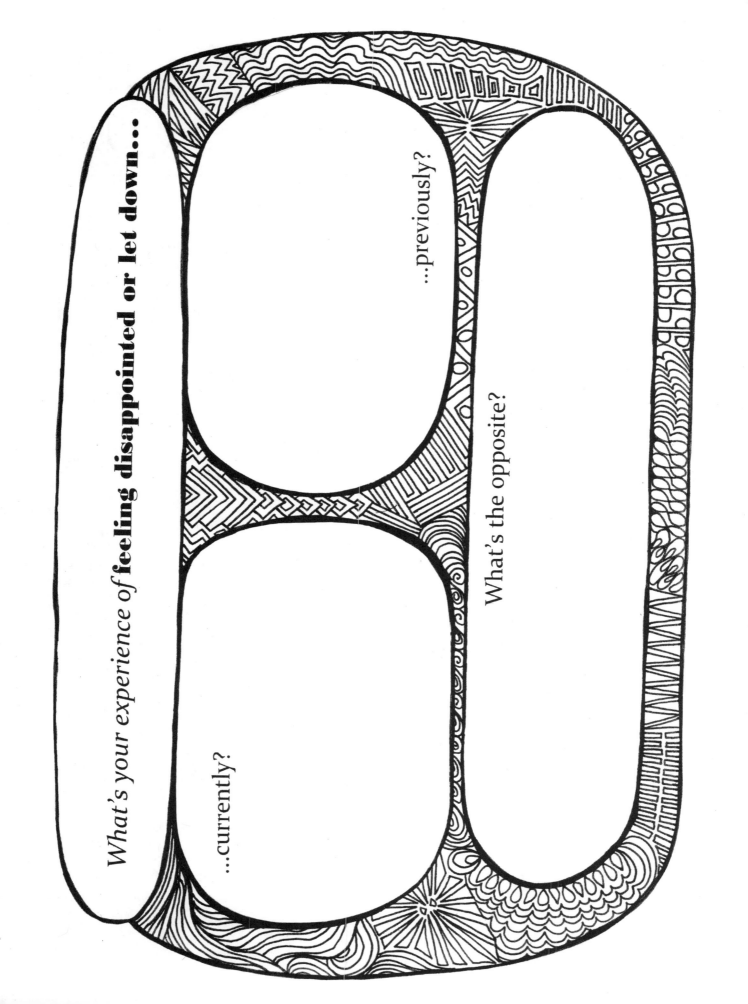

What's your experience of **feeling disappointed or let down**...

...currently?

...previously?

What's the opposite?

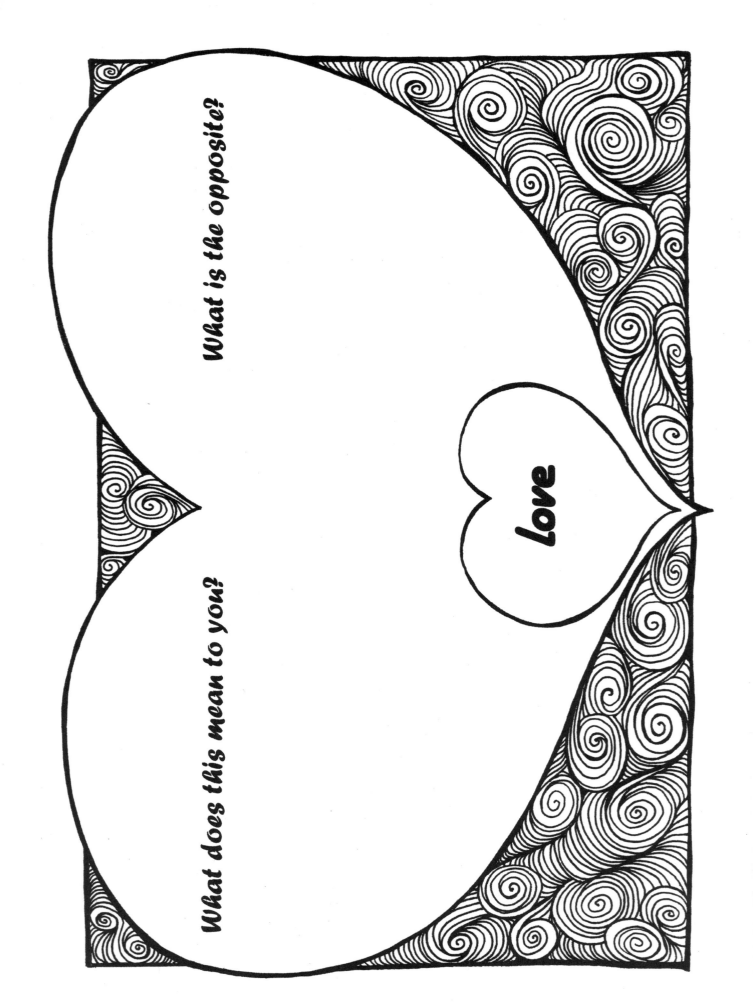

What is the opposite?

What does this mean to you?

love

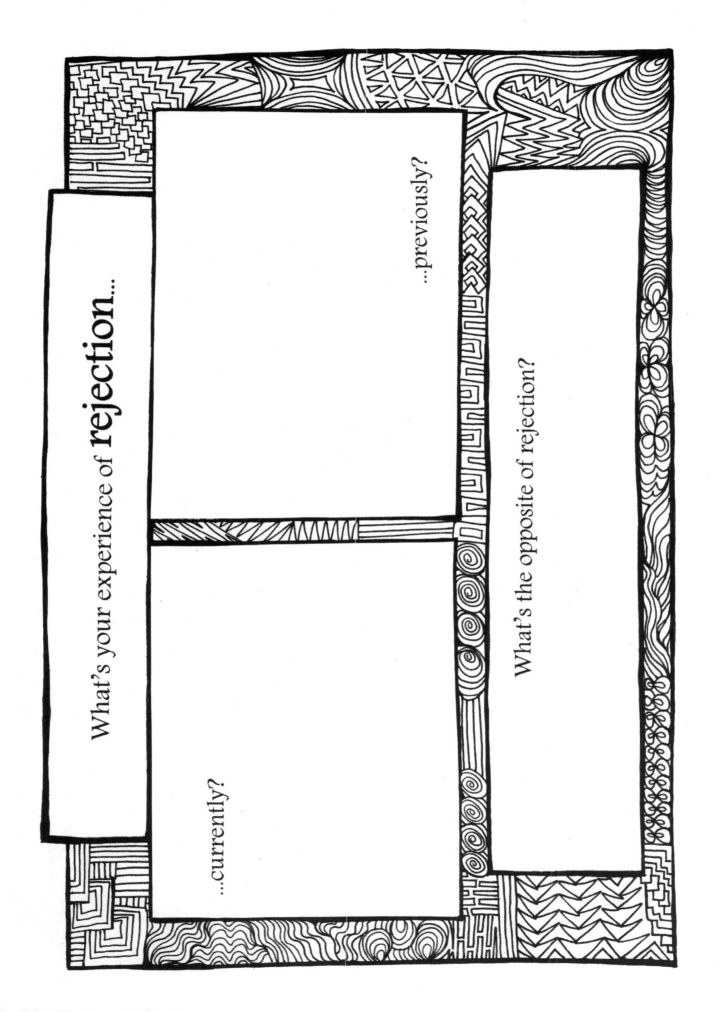

What's your experience of **rejection**...

...previously?

...currently?

What's the opposite of rejection?

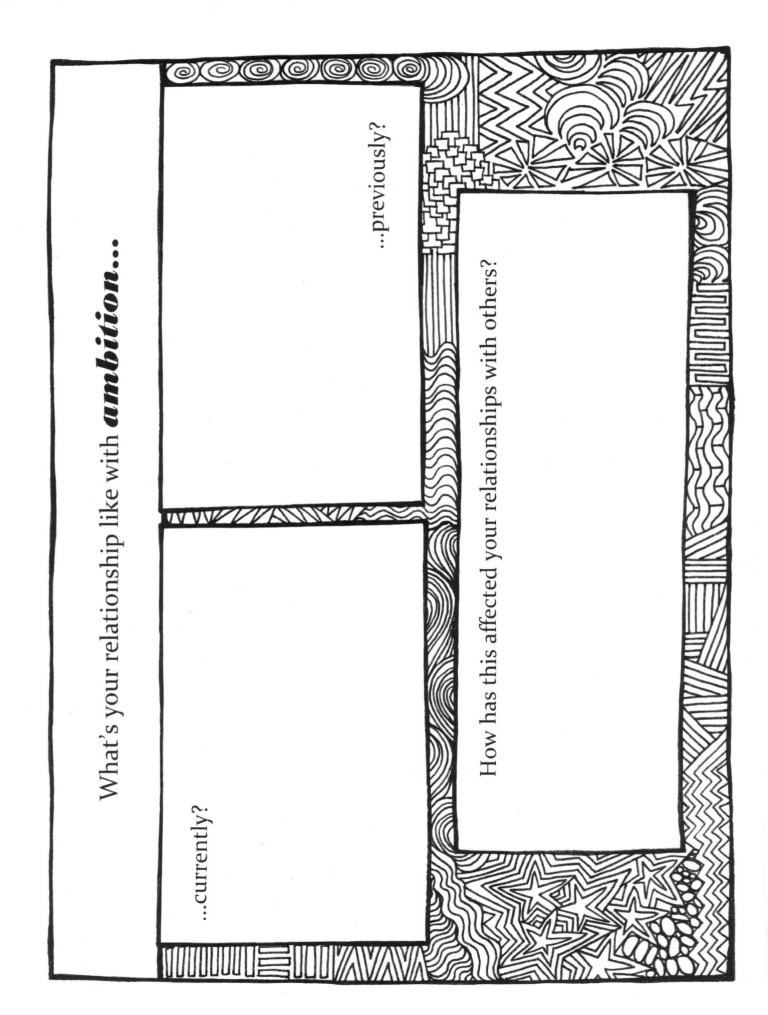

What's your relationship like with *ambition*...

...currently?

...previously?

How has this affected your relationships with others?

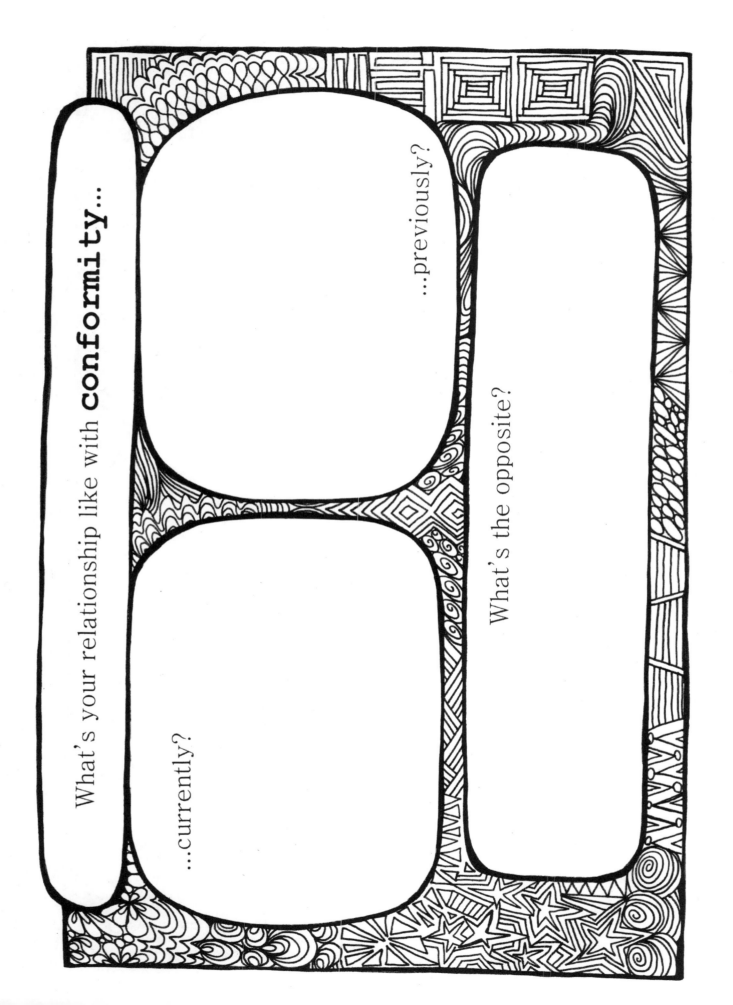

What's your relationship like with **conformity**...

...currently?

...previously?

What's the opposite?

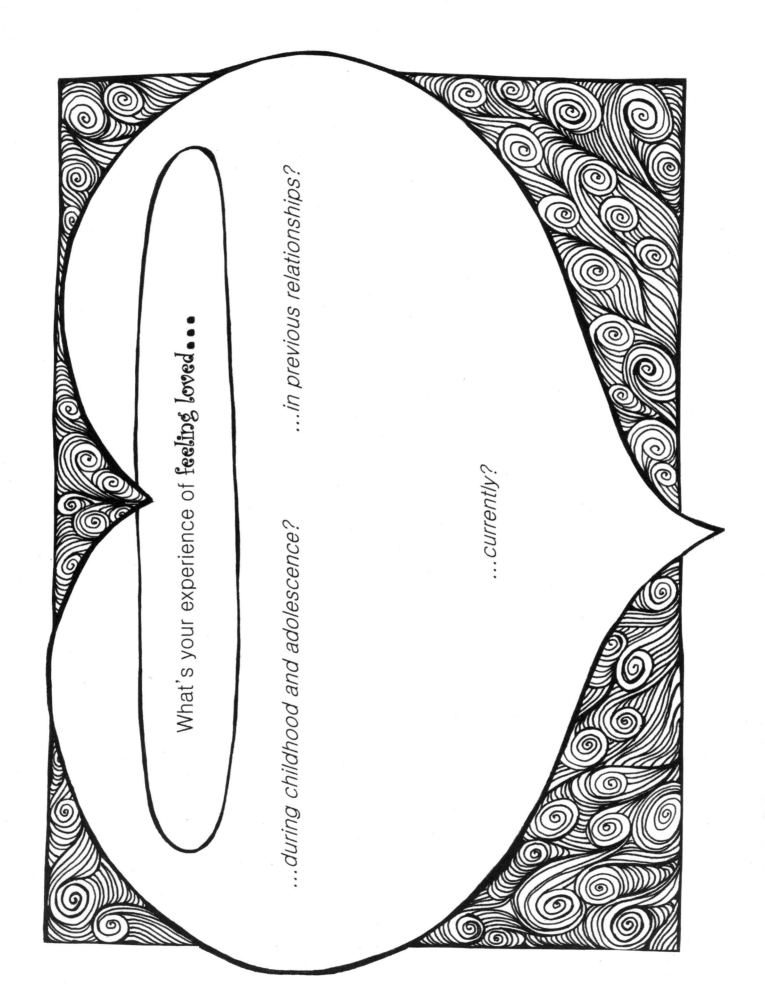

What's your experience of *feeling loved*...

...during childhood and adolescence?

...in previous relationships?

...currently?

What's your relationship like with your *favourite pastime/hobby…*

…currently?

…previously?

How has this affected your relationships with others?

How is your leisure time currently spent?

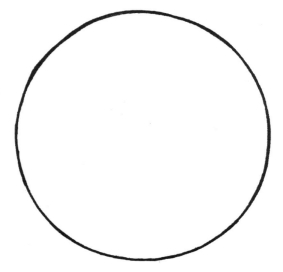

Divide the circle into slices of individual, couple and family time.

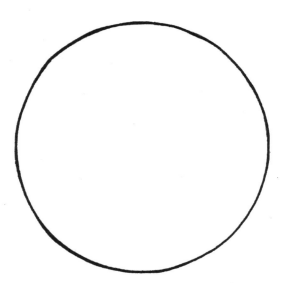

Would you prefer it to be different?

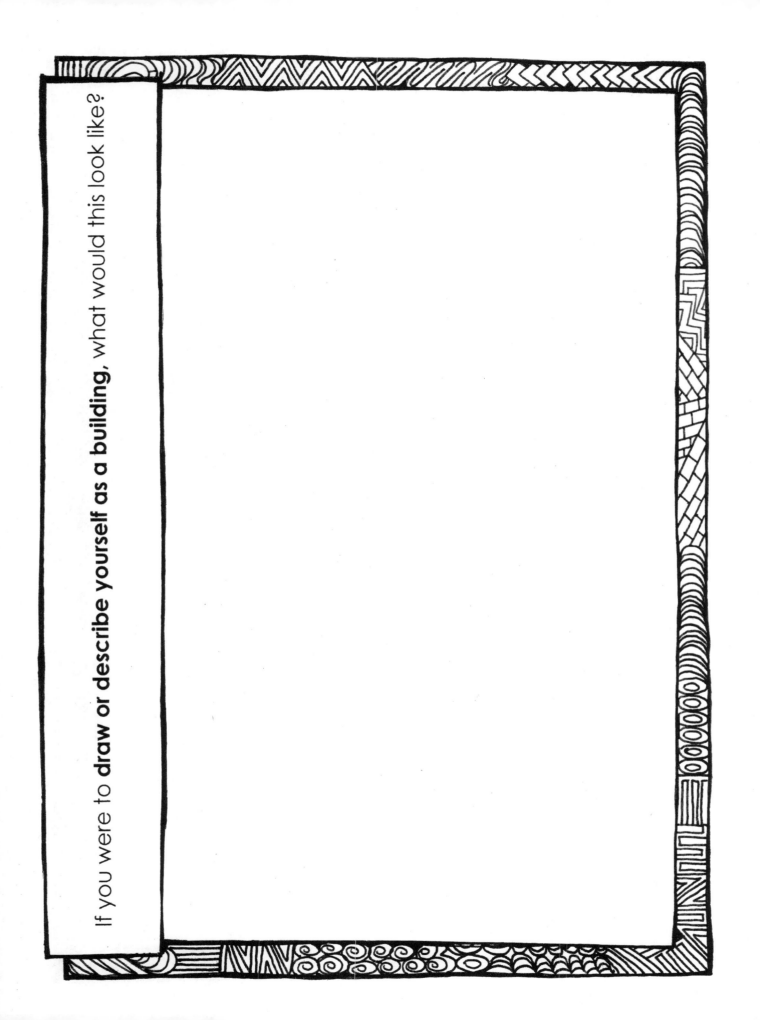

If you were to **draw or describe yourself as a building,** what would this look like?

(1) The **problem** is _____

Write a few words or draw a picture to describe the main characteristics of this problem.

(2) What are the effects and influences of this problem within these areas of your life?

Myself/My identity

Work/School

Home

(3) How do you feel about these; are any of these influences and effects OK with you?

Myself/My identity

Work/School

Home

Why do you think this is?

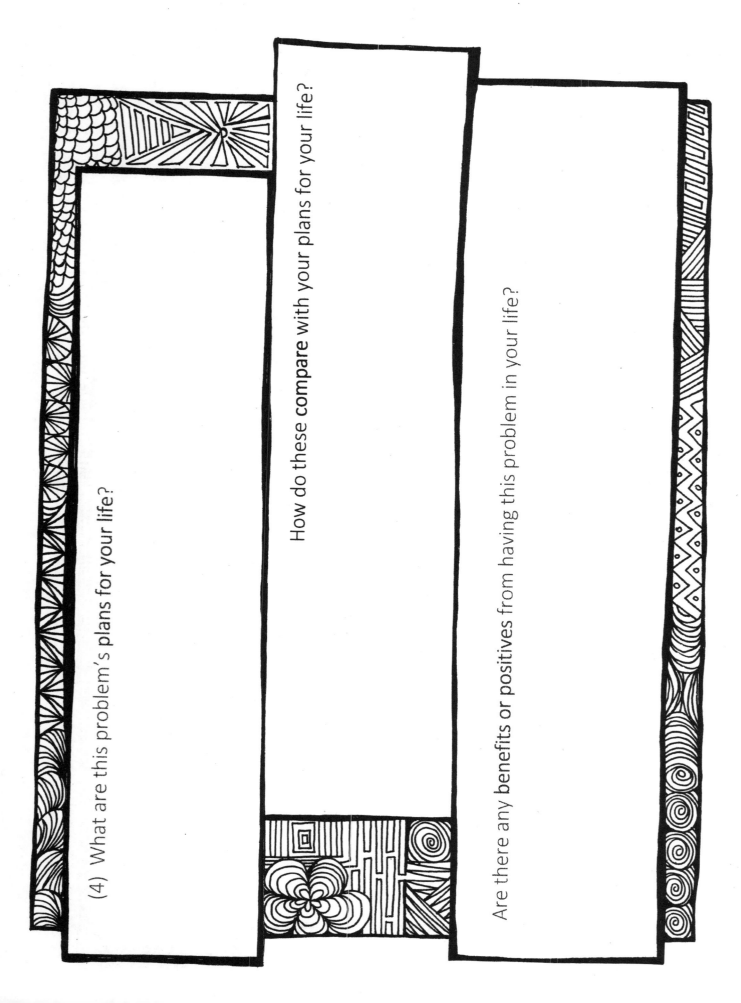

(4) What are this problem's plans for your life?

How do these **compare** with your plans for your life?

Are there any **benefits** or positives from having this problem in your life?

(5) What are the resources or strengths which could be developed, to free yourself from having

this problem in your life?

(6) Write a few words or draw a picture to describe the main characteristics of these strengths and resources.

Chapter 2

Couple Relationships

There are many approaches used in couple therapy today. The worksheets in this chapter have been developed from some of the theories informing these different approaches, mainly psychodynamic, systemic and cognitive behavioural. They can be helpful for individuals wanting to focus on relationship issues, or for couples to use them, either together or separately. Some focus on behavioural patterns, some are helpful for couples in recognising their emotional needs, and others focus on beliefs and expectations in relation to intimate partner relationships and roles. Others are for exploring and identifying potential areas for change.

In long-term relationships it can become challenging to maintain a balance between feeling a strong sense of being a part of a couple within that relationship and simultaneously experiencing a defined sense of self. This dilemma about boundaries is explored in great depth by Jurg Willi, in his book *Couples in Collusion* (1977). He describes the boundary in between a couple as intradyadic and the boundary around a couple as extradyadic. Problems can develop with individual identity or couple identity if these boundaries are too rigid.

There are a few worksheets in this chapter which aim to focus on exploring these ideas and people's experiences of boundaries. Often people can feel a great sense of belonging within a relationship and yet their sense of self becomes subsumed, or they can maintain a strong individual identity whilst there is a lack of a sense of belonging.

Theoretical perspectives
Psychodynamic theory

Attachment theory has had great influence in psychodynamic ways of thinking since the middle of the last century and the work of John Bowlby, who incorporated psychoanalytical ideas with systemic views. As mentioned in Chapter 1, in relation to our sense of identity, these ideas focus on how our experiences throughout infancy and childhood, in terms of the care and attention we received, influence the beliefs and expectations we have of and about ourselves and others in adulthood. Bowlby believed that these and an early bonding with a caregiver were fundamental to healthy social attachments later on in life, and these unconscious processes could be problematic if we had unresolved conflicts about them. Writing about this in *John Bowlby and Attachment Theory*, Jeremy Holmes explores the impact that attachment theory has had in adult psychotherapy practice in recent decades. He summarises the basic premise that 'a securely attached child will store an internal working model of a responsive and loving, reliable caregiver, and of a self that is worthy of love and attention and will bring these assumptions to bear on all other relationships' (1993, pp.78–79).

The idea of an internal model (Craik 1943) was developed by Bowlby into a 'working' internal model. These psychoanalytical perspectives were then incorporated into developments by Beck, Rush and Shaw (1979) with cognitive therapy ideas to do with how we build up a set of models about ourselves and others, which emerge from our experiences in childhood of repetitive interactional patterns with those around us (Holmes 1993).

Cognitive and integrative behavioural therapy

The aim of some worksheets is to bring out into the open discussions about how we think and the constructed ideas and beliefs we have about ourselves and others. Cognitions impact on our moods, interactions and ultimately the quality of our relationships. Often we have thoughts and beliefs about ourselves and our partners without fully realising the whole essence of them, so some worksheets aim to focus on bringing these into the open. It can also be helpful to explore the realistic nature of these, as described by Hewison, Clulow and Drake, in *Couple Therapy for Depression: A Clinician's Guide to Integrative Practice* (2014, p.18): 'From clinical work with couples it is clear that the boundaries between internal and external realities can easily become blurred.' So it can be incredibly valuable to check out the validity of certain beliefs.

Proponents of integrative behavioural couple therapy (Jacobson and Christensen 1996) suggest some questions that can 'help clarify what lies at the heart of a couple's concerns and their motivation for change' (Hewison et al. 2014, p.74). Two worksheets ('Our strengths as a couple' and 'How committed are you to this relationship') have been developed in direct response to some these questions, which are:

How distressed is each of the partners?

How committed are they to their relationship?

What issues divide them?

What are the strengths that hold them together as a couple?

Some worksheets here aim to help identify what a person's beliefs are about what constitutes a particular role and how these interact with the behaviour and beliefs of the other person (in that role). Problems often arise when there are significant differences between these and the ideas of the other person. In addition to the roles ascribed to an individual because of gender or inter-generational position, there are the roles that are independent of these and that refer to behavioural attributions, for example, 'the peacemaker' or 'the scapegoat'. Hewison *et al.* (2014, p.74) write, 'The ways partners behave together will provide information about the implicit allocation of roles between them… These can help identify recurring patterns of interaction that are causing problems.'

Systemic theory

One of the basic premises of applying systemic thinking to relationships is to foster an understanding with couples that there is 'a shared systemic understanding of the difficulties without laying disproportionate blame on one partner' (Carr 2012, p.371). This obviously precludes any partners within a domestically abusive relationship. In *Family Therapy: Concepts, Process and Practice*, Carr continues by saying that 'this shared understanding should allow partners to empathise with each other and see that they are both trapped in a destructive problem system to which they both make a contribution' (2012, p.371).

For therapy with couples, systems theory can 'provide a way of connecting past with current patterns of relationship, gender roles with social expectations of these roles and behaviours with meaning' (Rivett and Street 2009, p.267). Some of the worksheets in this chapter focus on the interactional patterns between partners. These patterns are considered in the context of the relationship, and it can be useful and empowering for people 'to see that they are not the pattern, and they have the capacity to create new patterns between them' (Hewison *et al.* 2014, p.110). The ideas for these worksheets came about from the approach described in *Couple Therapy for Depression: A Clinician's Guide to Integrative Practice* (2014), which was developed from the work of Christensen and Jacobson (1996, 2000).

Influences from the wider system of extended family or community can add pressure or be a source of support for partner relationships, including influential cultural aspects. As stated by Hewison *et al.*, 'The ecology of a couple in terms of social, cultural, religious, and economic influences plays a large part in defining roles and normative behaviour for couples' (2014, p.75). Some worksheets help explore these aspects and how life changes have impacted on partner relationships. These could be external influences from wider systems or intra-psychic changes within the partners themselves.

Relational issues are often about the balance of power between the two partners. Some worksheets aim to promote people in exploring these ideas about power within their roles of the relationship. An unbalanced distribution of power between partners can have a hugely negative impact on the relationship and the wellbeing of partners. Through helping couples to renegotiate their roles within a relationship, this can bring about a realignment of power imbalances (Carr 2012).

What does being **a partner** mean to you?

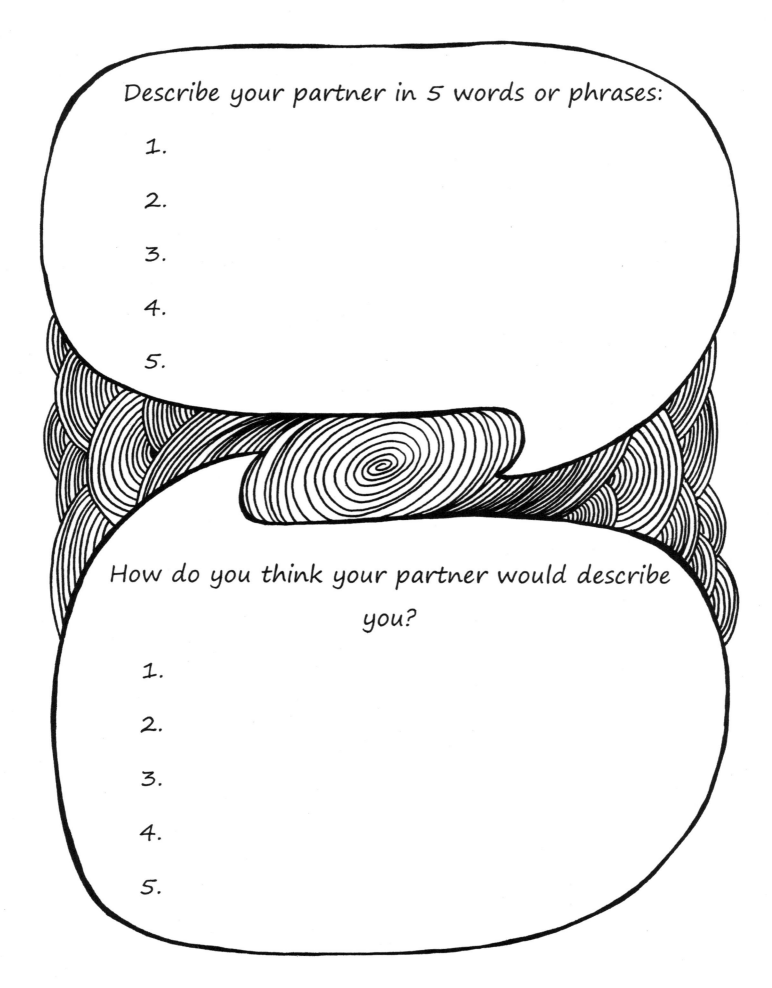

Describe your partner in 5 words or phrases:

1.

2.

3.

4.

5.

How do you think your partner would describe you?

1.

2.

3.

4.

5.

What is your idea of a **wife**?

What is your idea of a husband?

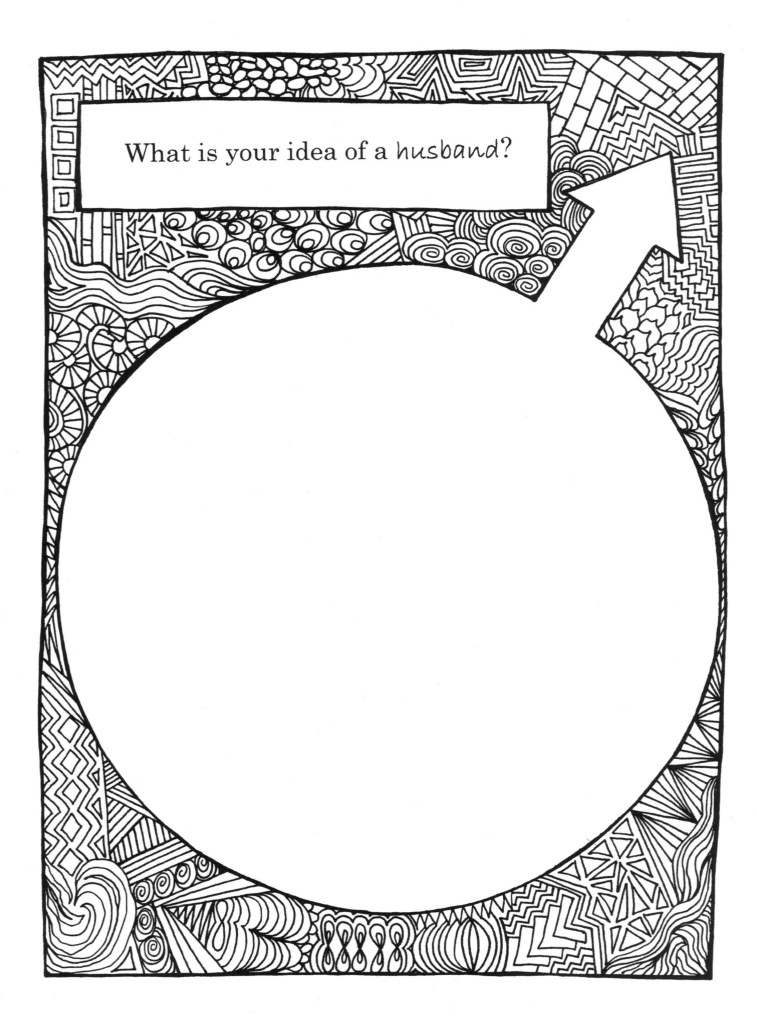

What are the **5 most important aspects to you**, in a relationship? (e.g. shared sense of humour, intellectual stimulation)

What **percentage** are each of these currently being met?

In these areas of responsibility, what is **the percentage division** between you and your partner?

	You	Partner
Daily domestic tasks		
Earning income		
Childcare		
Finances (paying bills, etc.)		
Shared leisure time		
DIY		
Pets		

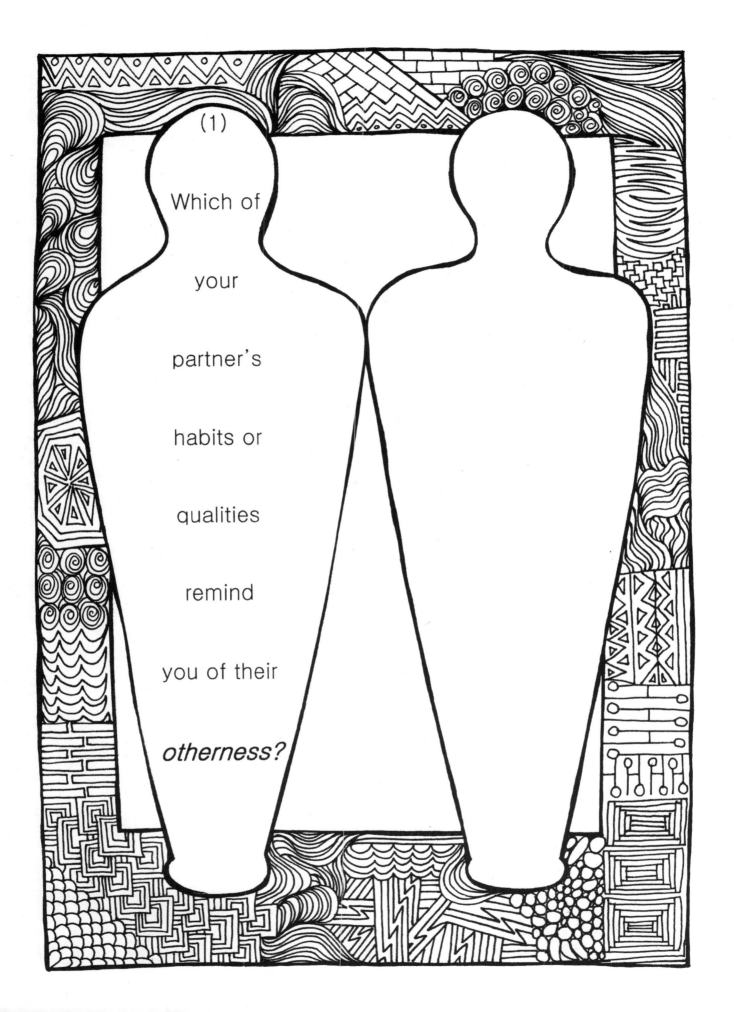

(1)

Which of

your

partner's

habits or

qualities

remind

you of their

otherness?

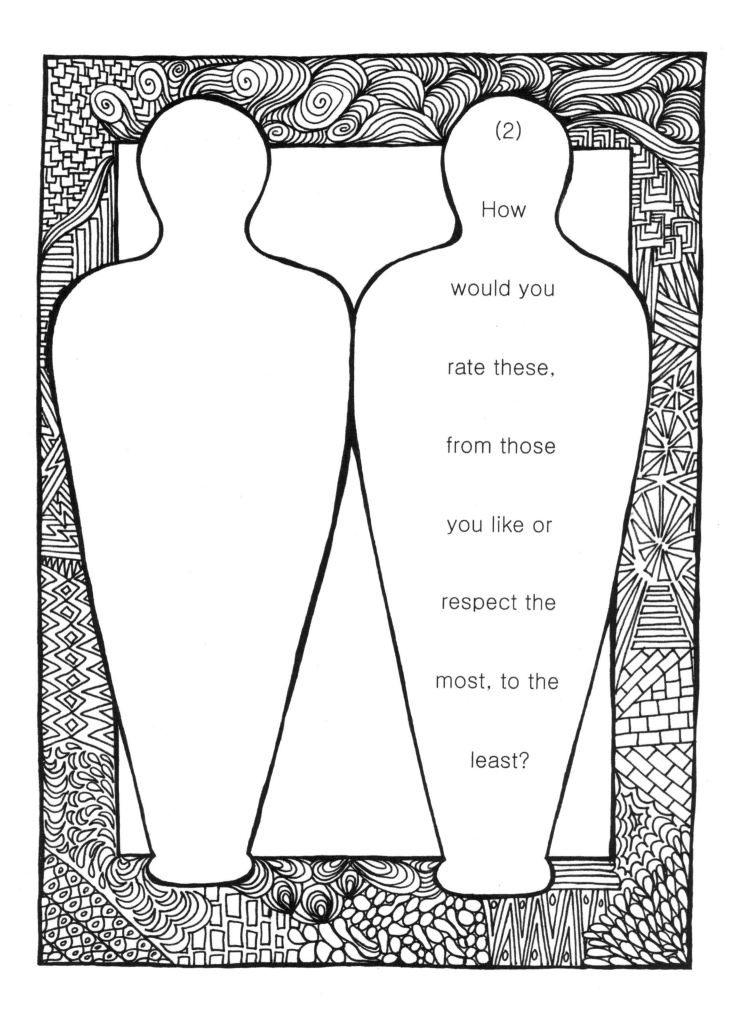

(2)

How

would you

rate these,

from those

you like or

respect the

most, to the

least?

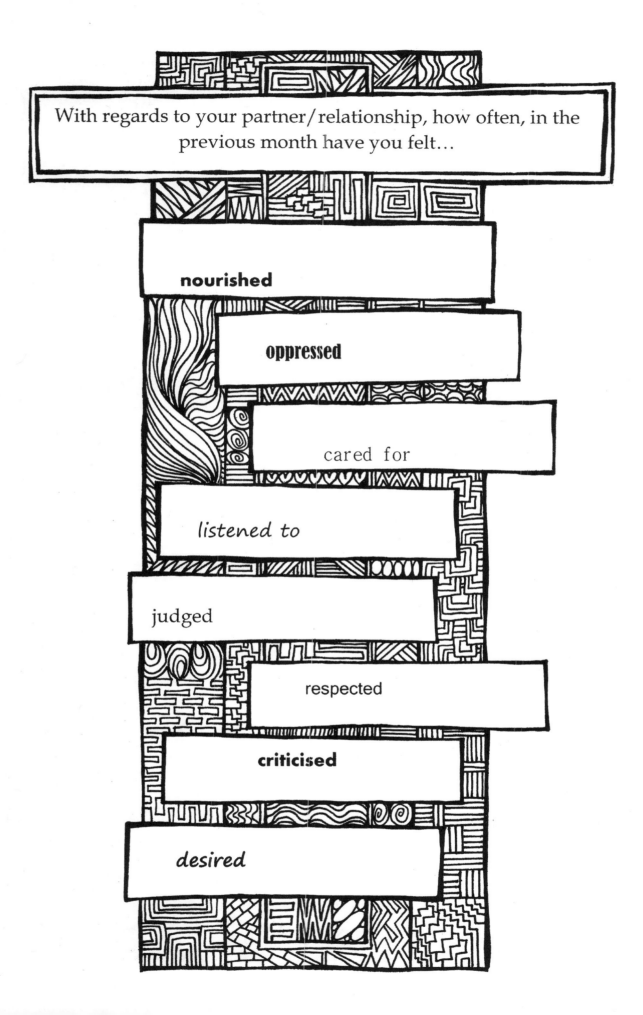

With regards to your partner/relationship, how often, in the
previous month have you felt…

nourished

oppressed

cared for

listened to

judged

respected

criticised

desired

If you met your current partner for the *very first time* today, how would you respond?

Would you want to commit to being in a relationship with them?

Would you find them attractive?

Would you want to spend more time together?

How do they fit in with your ideal vision of a partner?

Think of **10 inexpensive ways** you could let your partner know that you **love** them:

1.

2.

3.

4.

5.

6.

7.

8.

9.

10.

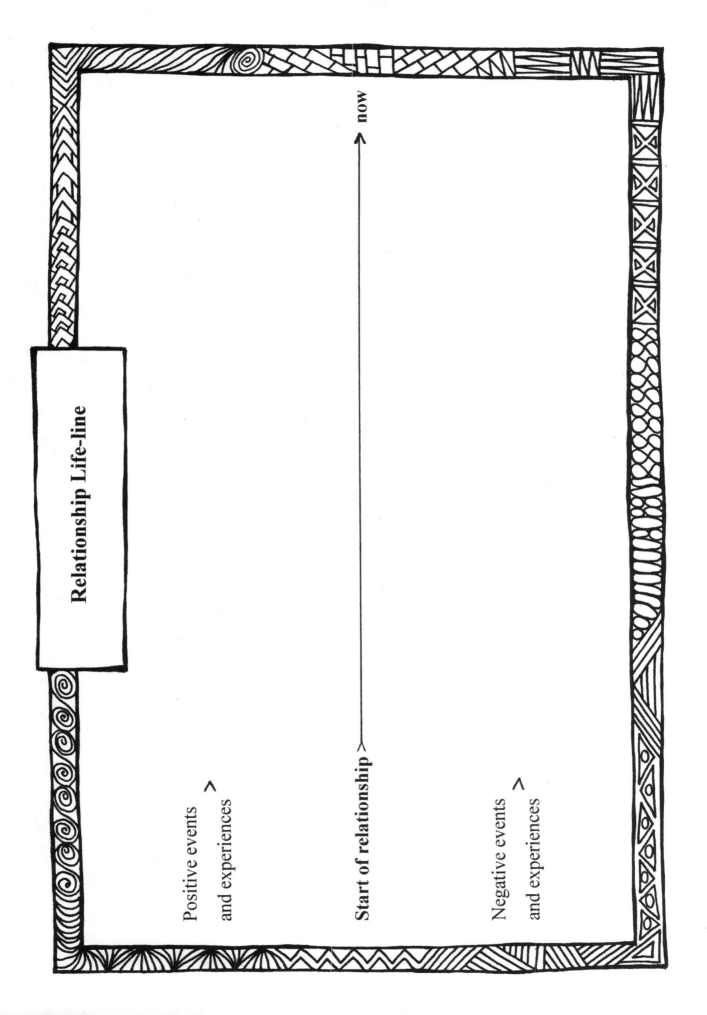

Relationship Life-line

Positive events
and experiences

Start of relationship ⟶ now

Negative events
and experiences

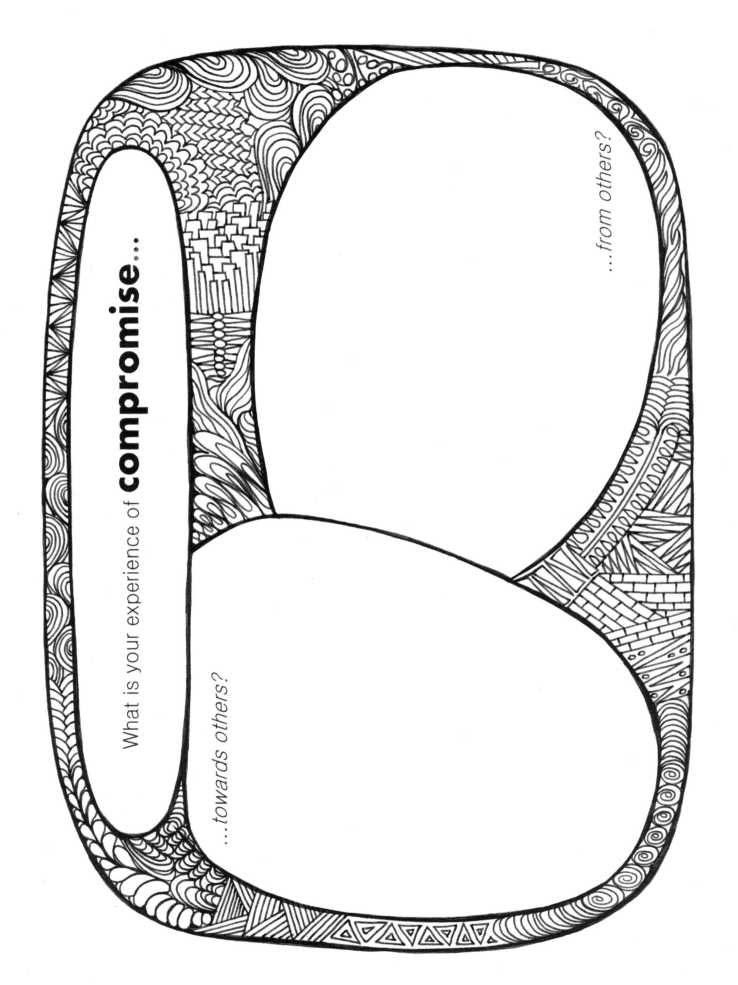

What is your experience of **compromise**...

...towards others?

...from others?

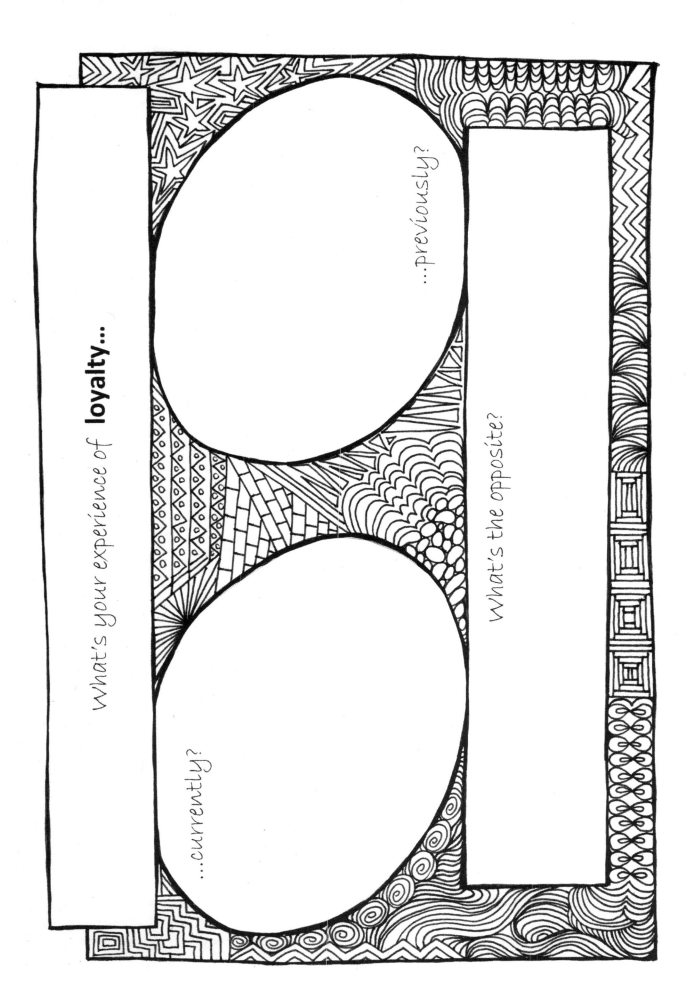

what's your experience of **loyalty**...

...previously?

...currently?

What's the opposite?

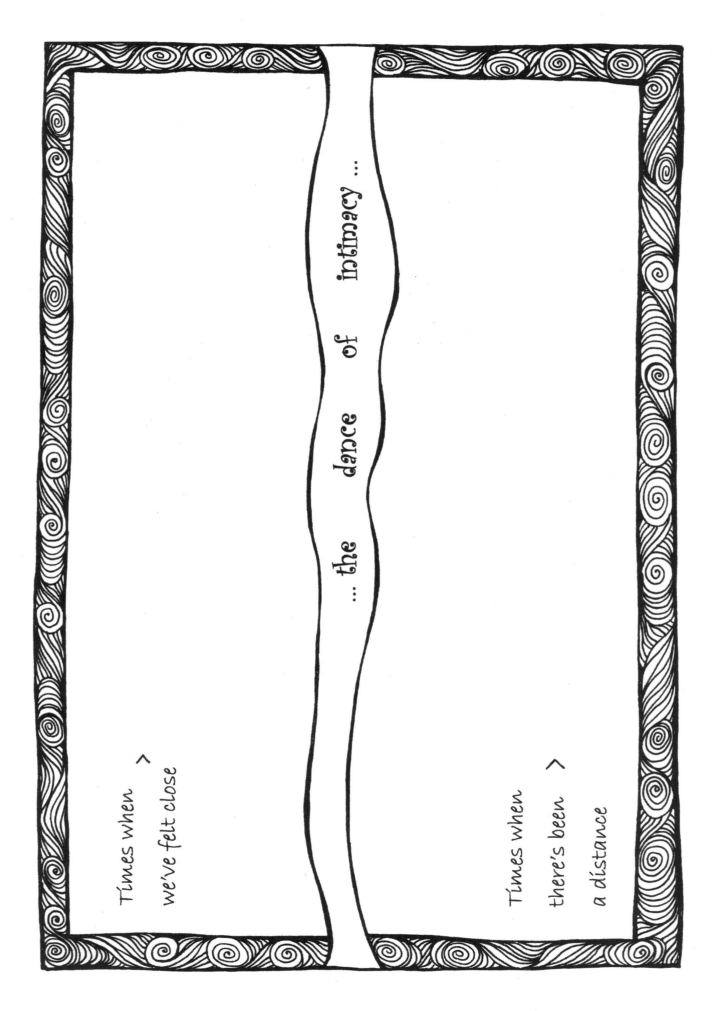

... the dance of intimacy ...

Times when > we've felt close

Times when > there's been a distance

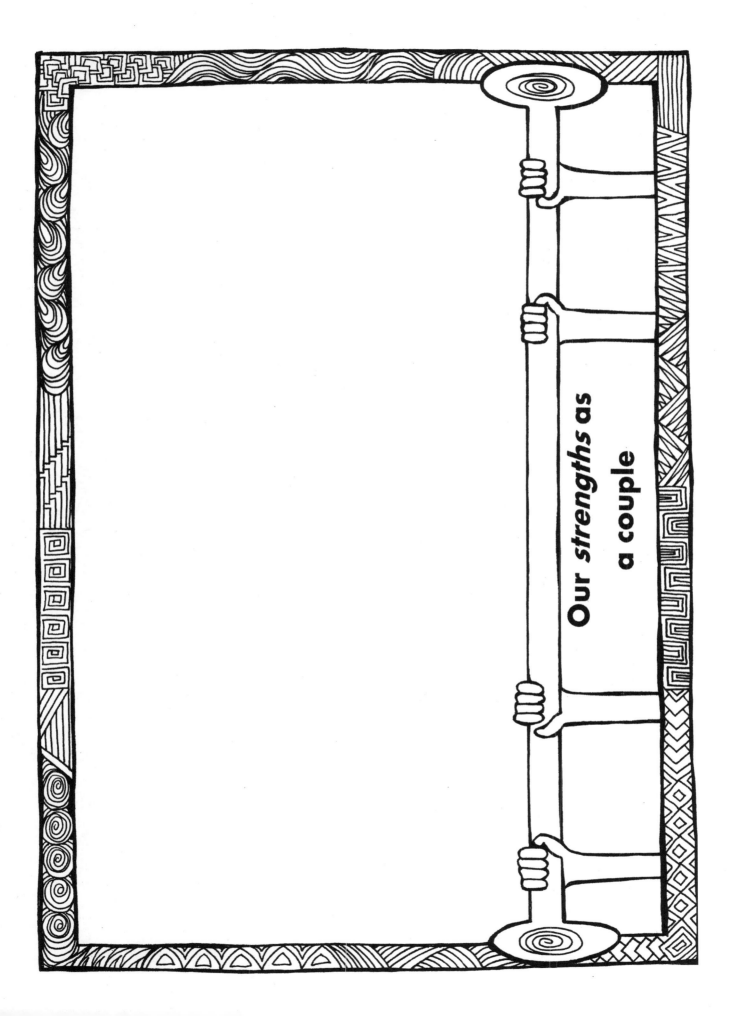

Our strengths as a couple

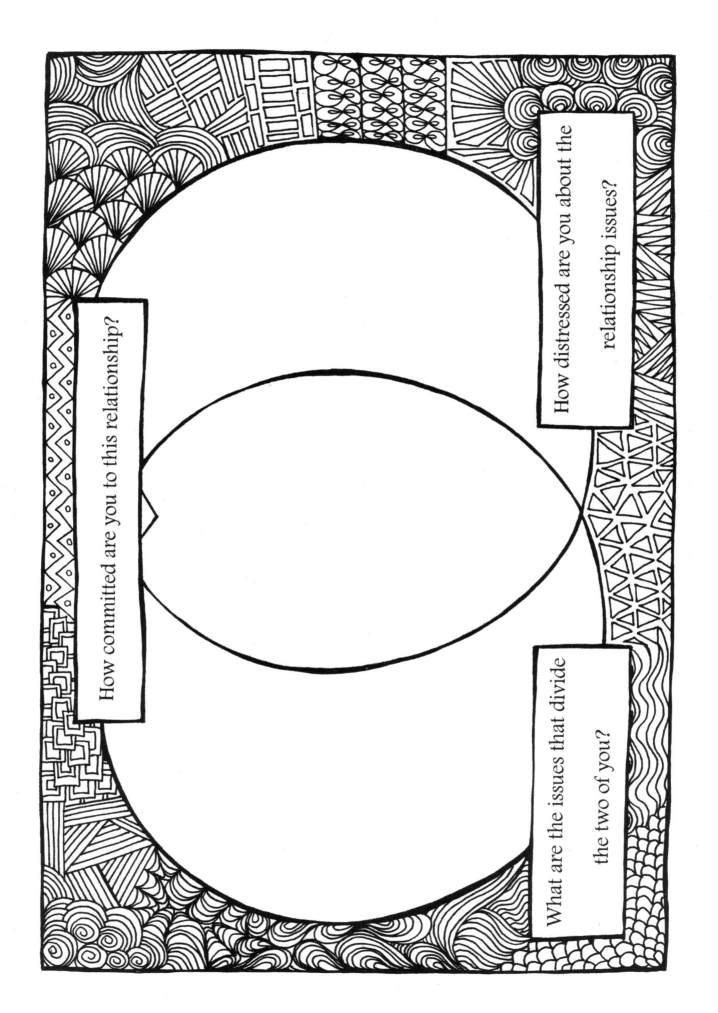

How distressed are you about the relationship issues?

How committed are you to this relationship?

What are the issues that divide the two of you?

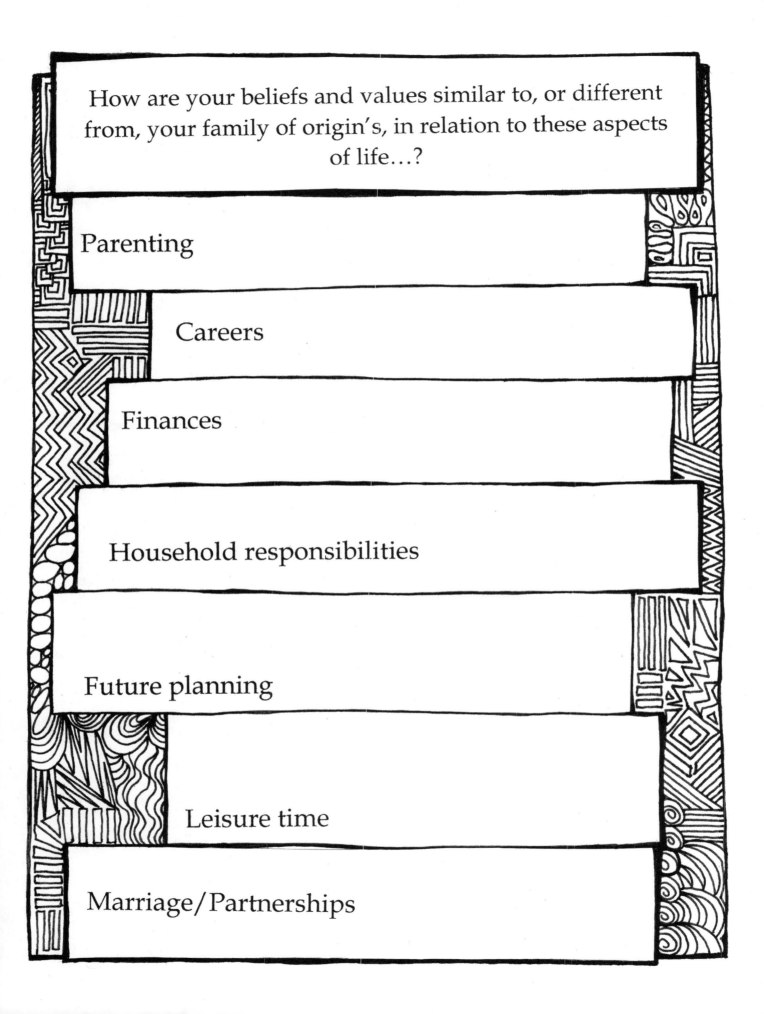

How are your beliefs and values similar to, or different from, your family of origin's, in relation to these aspects of life…?

Parenting

Careers

Finances

Household responsibilities

Future planning

Leisure time

Marriage/Partnerships

These 2 circles represent you and your partner:

If they were to represent the two of you in your relationship,

how would you place them?

Examples:

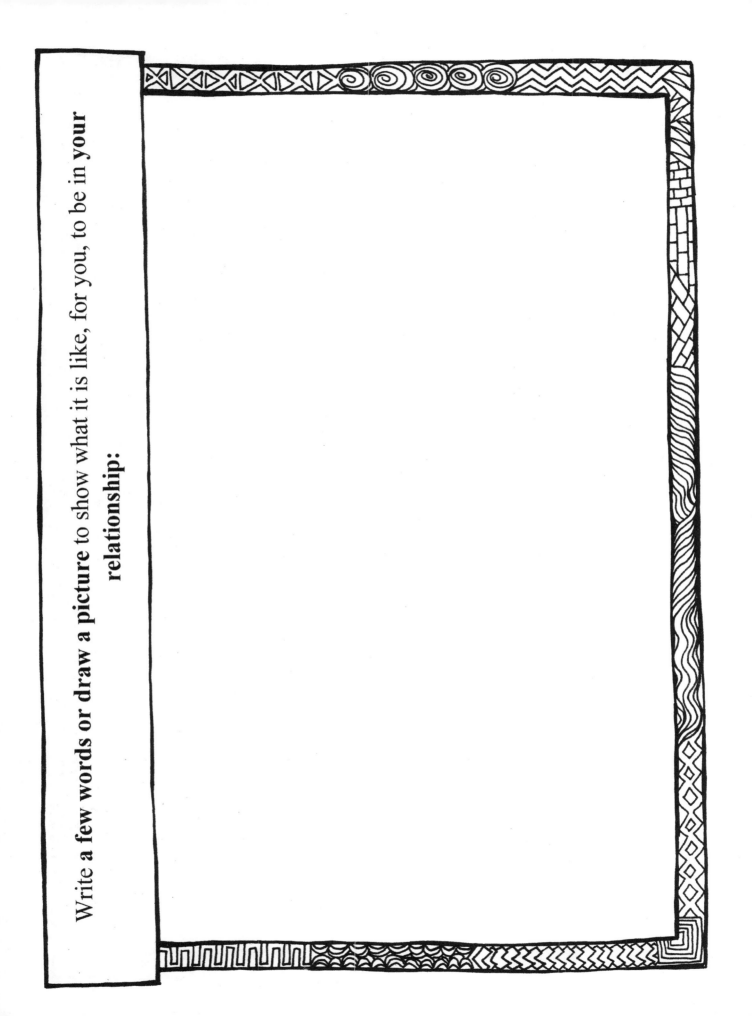

Write a few words or draw a picture to show what it is like, for you, to be in your relationship:

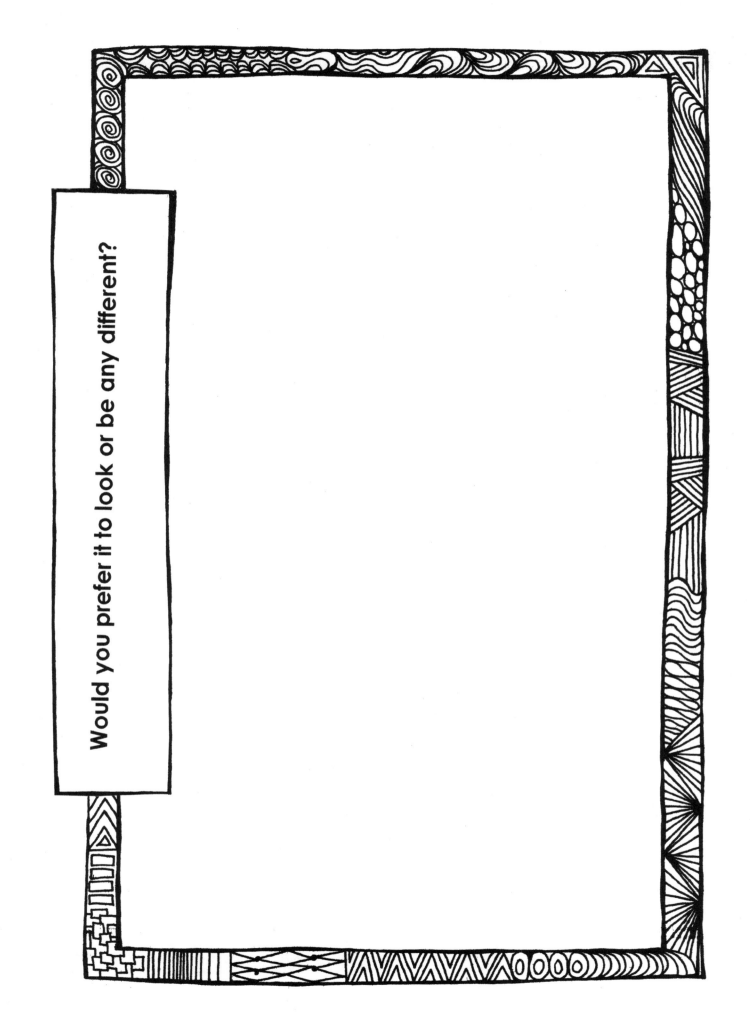

Would you prefer it to look or be any different?

You and your partner win a life-changing amount of money....

what do you do?

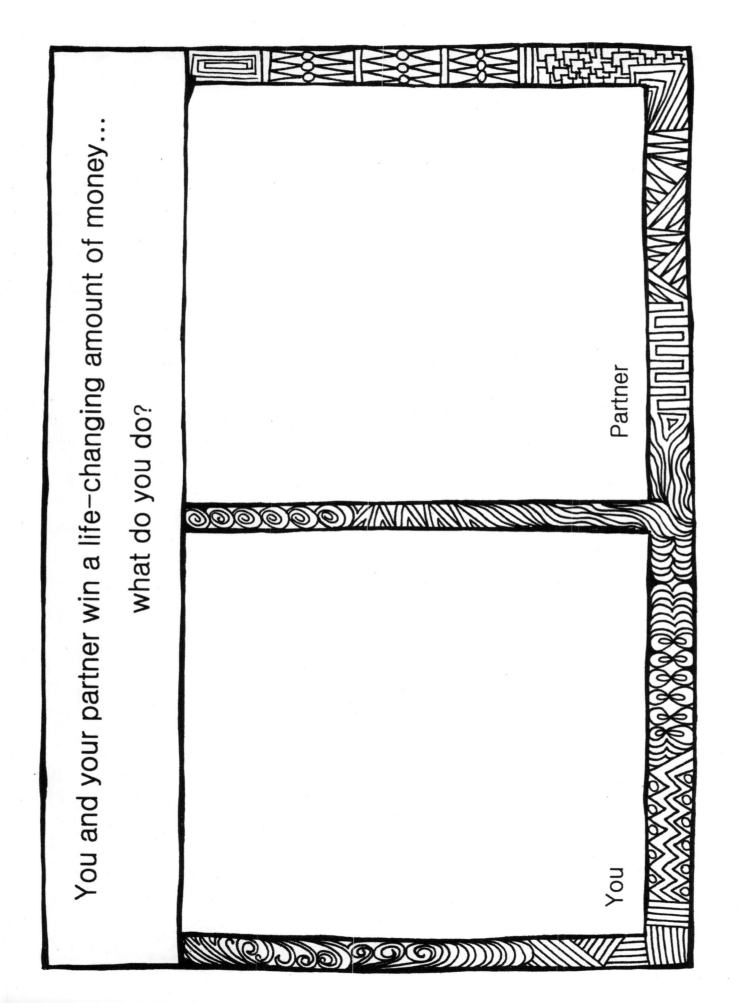

Partner

You

What's your idea of a lover?

Chapter 3

Family

Many of the worksheets in this chapter provide a focus point to help family members increase positive interactions with one another, with the aim of improving closeness, understanding and acceptance between family members.

Visual tools can be exceptionally useful when it comes to exploring and understanding intergenerational patterns. Drawing out these patterns can be helped by using the framework of a genogram. This is a widely used visual technique used in family and couple work and was standardised by the North American Primary Care Research Group in the early 1980s. The diagrams can show family history in a way that gives immediate insights into patterns and how problems may have evolved over time within the context of the family (McGoldrick 1999). Some worksheets here focus on providing visual explorations into patterns and dynamics between family members, and are directly developed from these ideas of a genogram's framework. Other creative tools, such as facilitating clients to use stones or buttons to demonstrate relational dynamics, have been influential in the development of some worksheets in this chapter.

The family task worksheet ('If you were to colour-in this picture…') was inspired by systemic family psychotherapist Paul Stockwell.

Theoretical perspectives
Systemic theory

Gregory Bateson was a pioneer when he applied the ideas of systems theory and cybernetics to the idea of families as natural systems. In *Steps to an Ecology of Mind* (1972, p.xxxii) he wrote: 'Mental process, ideas, communication, organisation, differentiation, pattern, and so on, are matters of form…form has been dramatically enriched by the discoveries of cybernetics and systems theory.' Families are seen as a system within the wider systems of extended family, communities, cultures and socio-political climates. There are subsystems within families, such as the parental system, or those defined gender or generation (Bateson 1972). All systems have permeable boundaries around them, which are defined by the individuals within that particular system (Rivett and Street 2009). Within a family, members are, to a certain extent, 'defined and maintained by circular interactional patterns of which they are a part' (Rivett and Street 2009, p.14).

Other worksheets in this chapter aim to inspire people in bringing about new information, to enlighten how they might resolve problems. This information is 'definable as a difference which makes a difference' (Bateson 1972, p.315) and could be focused around family members' beliefs, feelings or behaviours (Carr 2012). Bateson (1972) described the process of gaining more information as 'double description' and that 'if two descriptions are given of the same events, then the difference in perspectives provides news of difference, and this may help family systems to change so as to adapt to their problematic circumstances', as explained by Alan Carr in his book *Family Therapy: Concepts, Process and Practice* (Carr 2012, p.70).

Meanings and perspectives are key considerations in systemic thinking, and it can be helpful to focus on exploring 'the different ways people might understand an event, which reflects the fact they live in different contexts, but also how they order their different understandings the way they do…to clarify the "meanings of the meanings"…which determines why people see and understand what they do' (Campbell 1994, p.16). Many of the worksheets here aim for people to gain some clarification of the meanings we attach to experiences and events, and to act as platforms for conversations about them.

Cognitive behavioural therapy

Alan Carr, writing about the cyclical nature of negative cognitions in *Family Therapy: Concepts, Process and Practice*, believes that 'family members in distressed relationships engage in more negative interpersonal behaviour patterns, which are mutually reinforcing, and view each other in more negative terms' (2012, p.99). Some of the worksheets aim to identify unhelpful thoughts and beliefs which fuel less positive interactions and behaviour.

Draw a shape for each family member, placing each one in a position to represent some of the relational dynamics, such as closeness/distance.

Different sizes and colours can be helpful.

Here is an example:

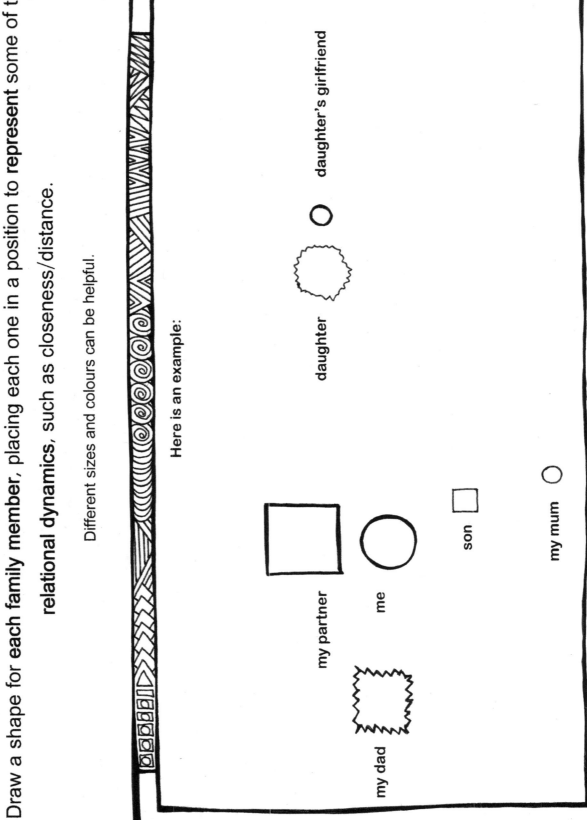

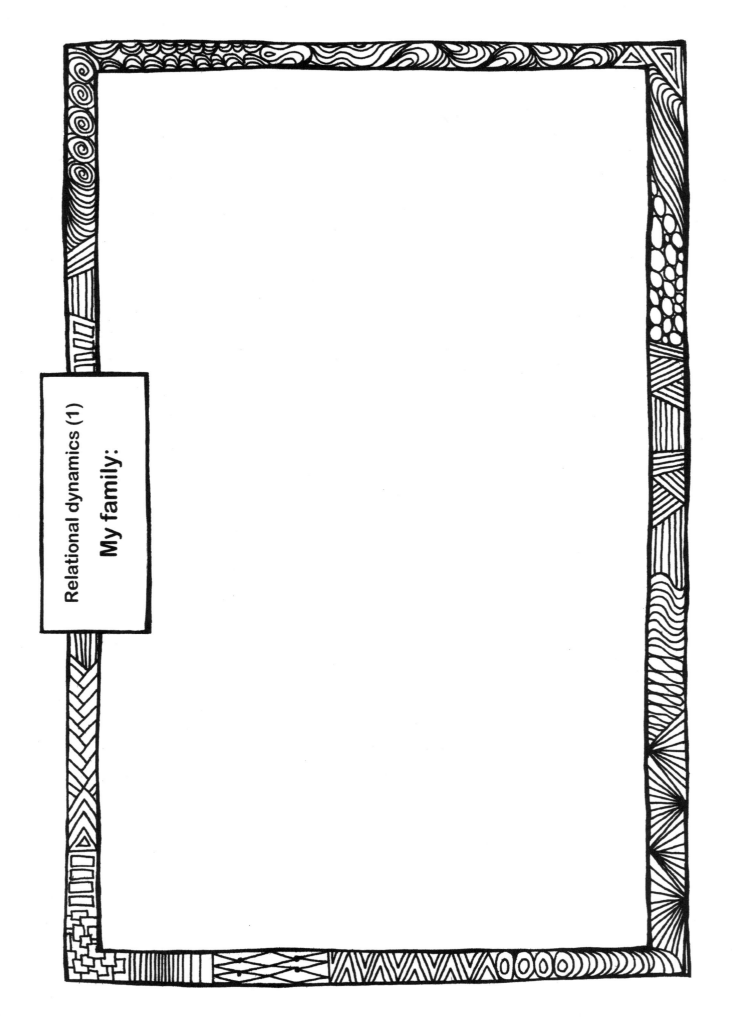

Relational dynamics (1)

My family:

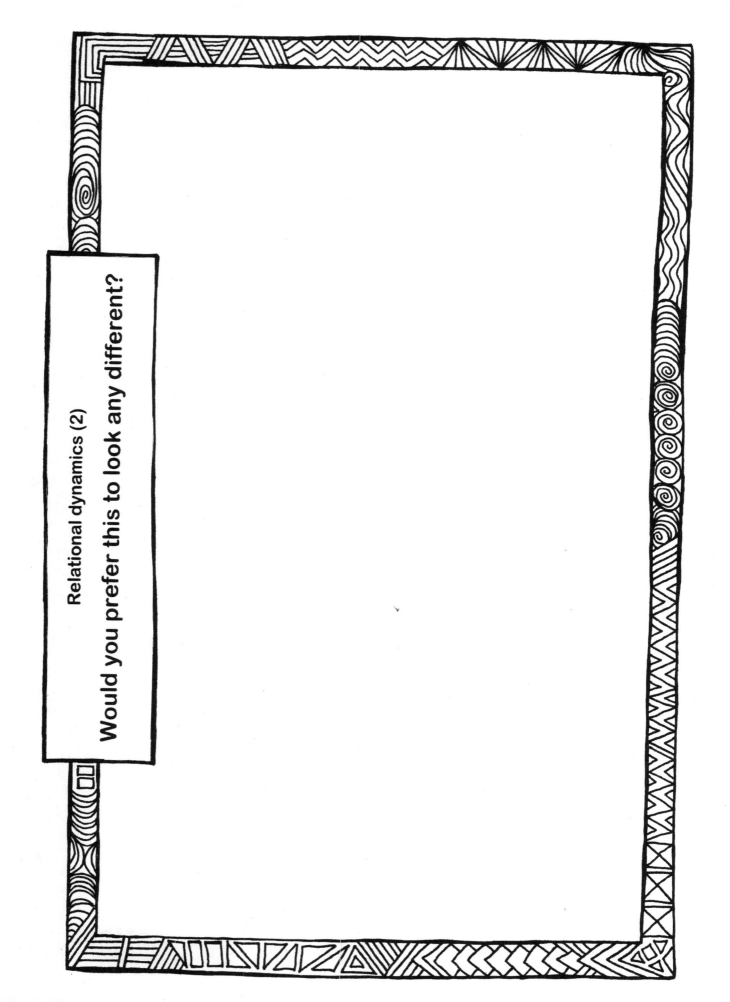

Relational dynamics (2)

Would you prefer this to look any different?

Relational dynamics (3)

How do you think your partner would draw the family?

What is your idea of a mother?

What is your idea of a **father**?

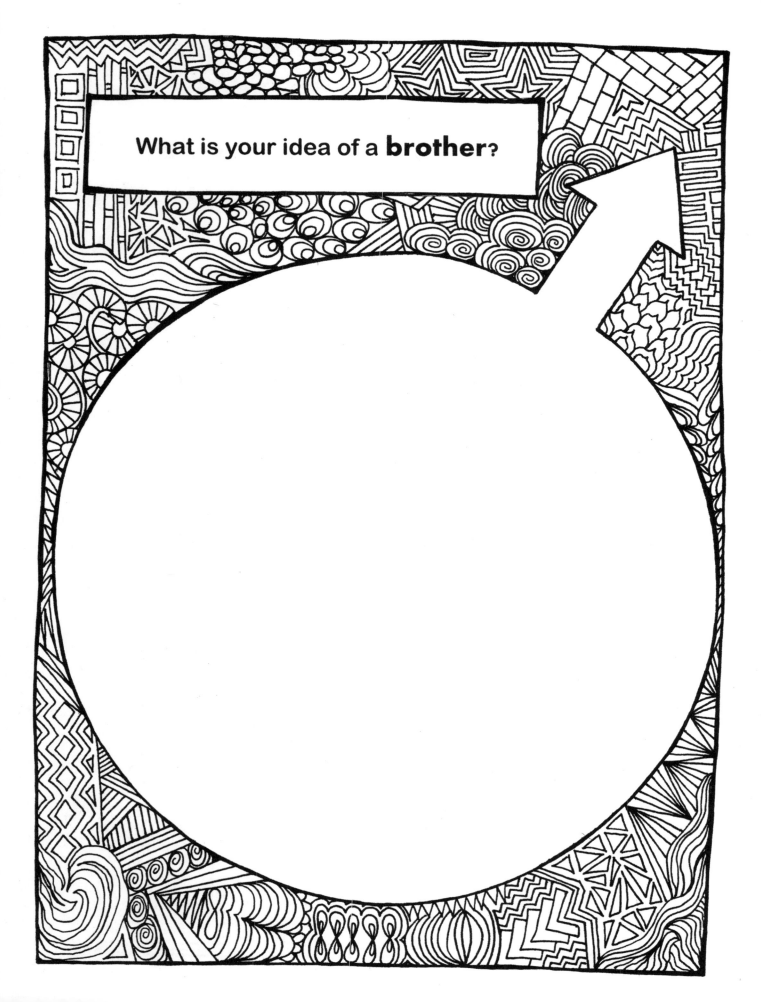

What is your idea of a **brother**?

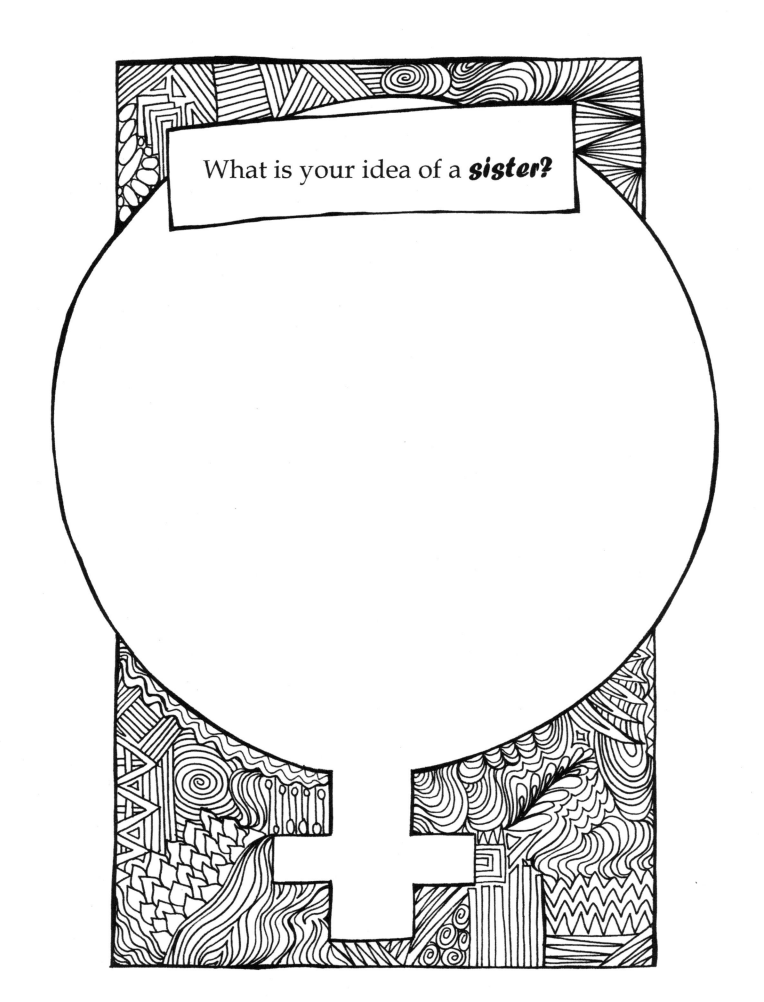

What is your idea of a **sister?**

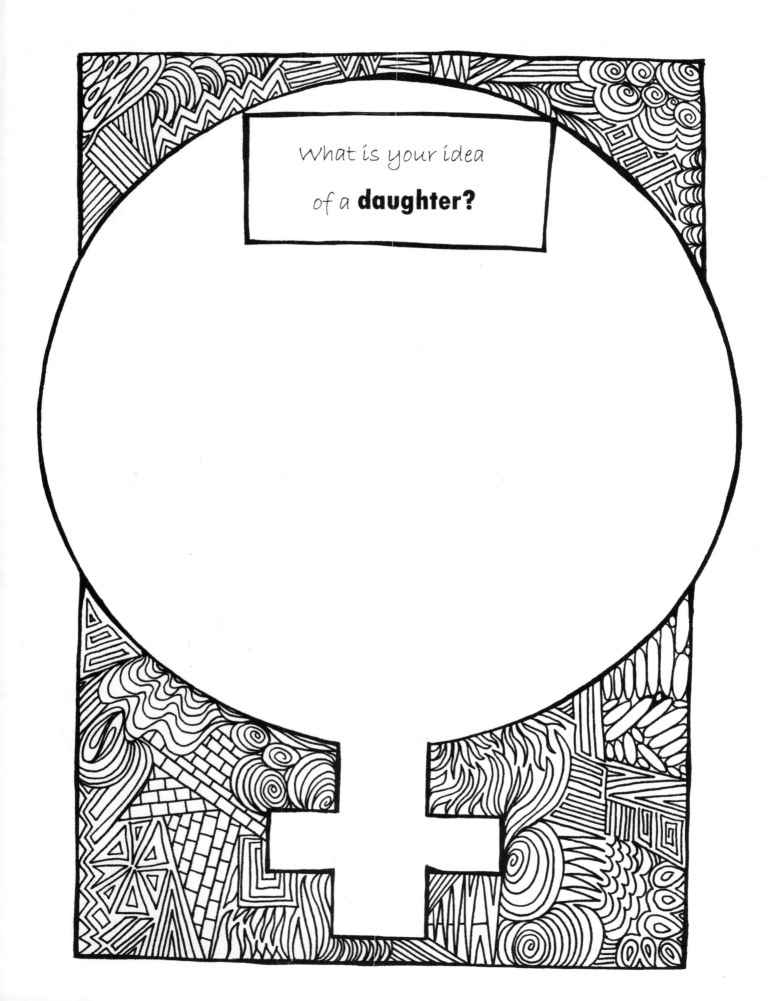

What is your idea

of a **daughter?**

What is your idea of a **son**?

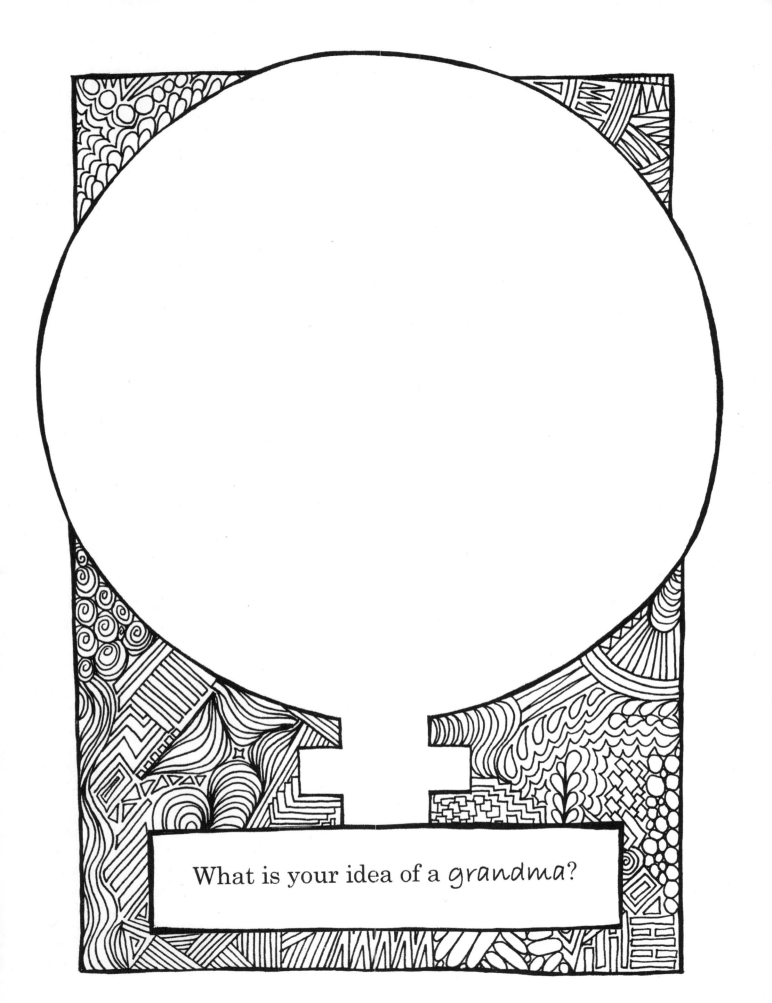

What is your idea of a *grandma*?

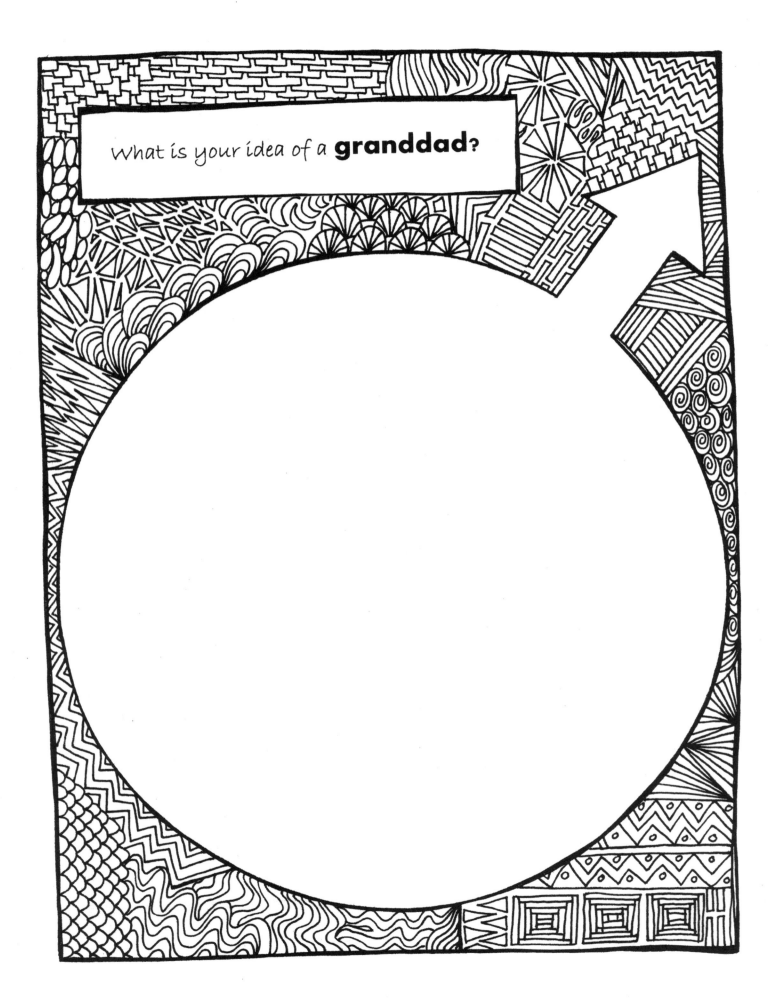

what is your idea of a **granddad?**

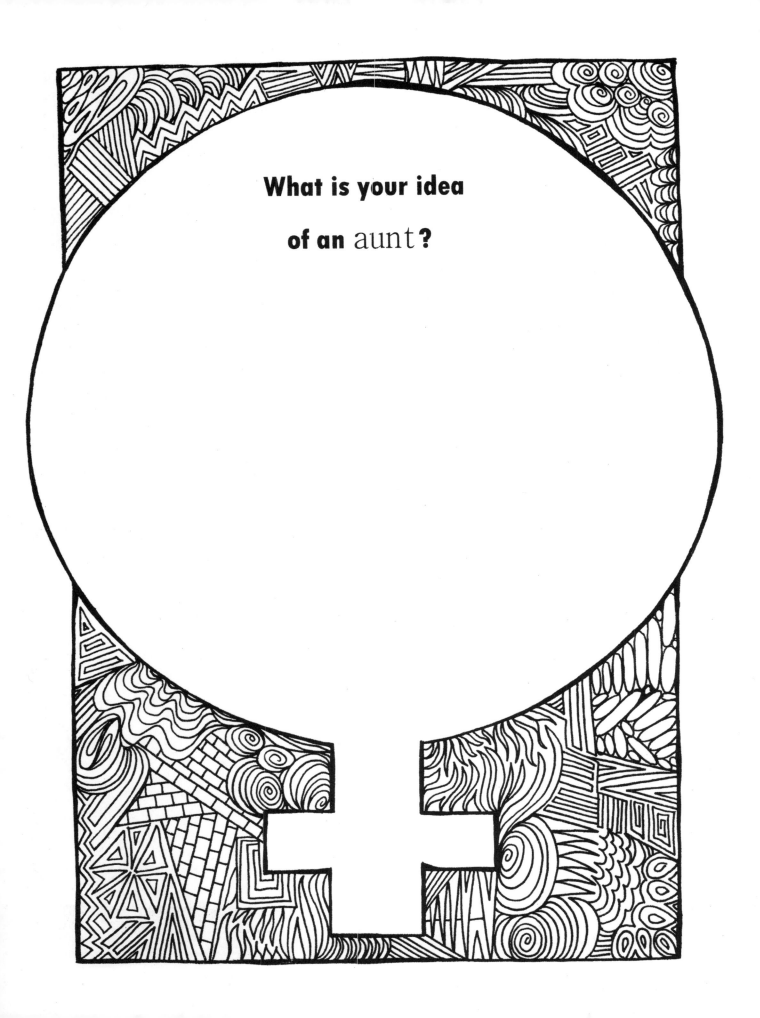

What is your idea

of an aunt **?**

What is your idea of an **uncle?**

What is your idea of a **step-dad?**

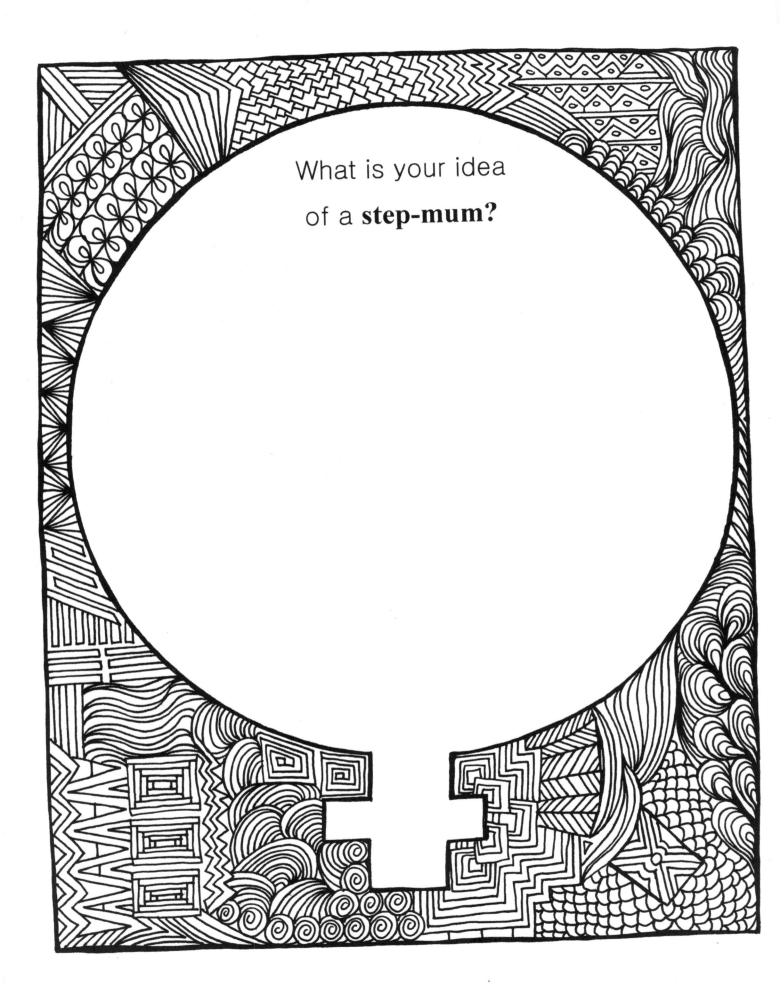

What is your idea

of a **step-mum?**

What is the balance of **autonomy and a sense of belonging** like in your family?

Sense of belonging

Autonomy

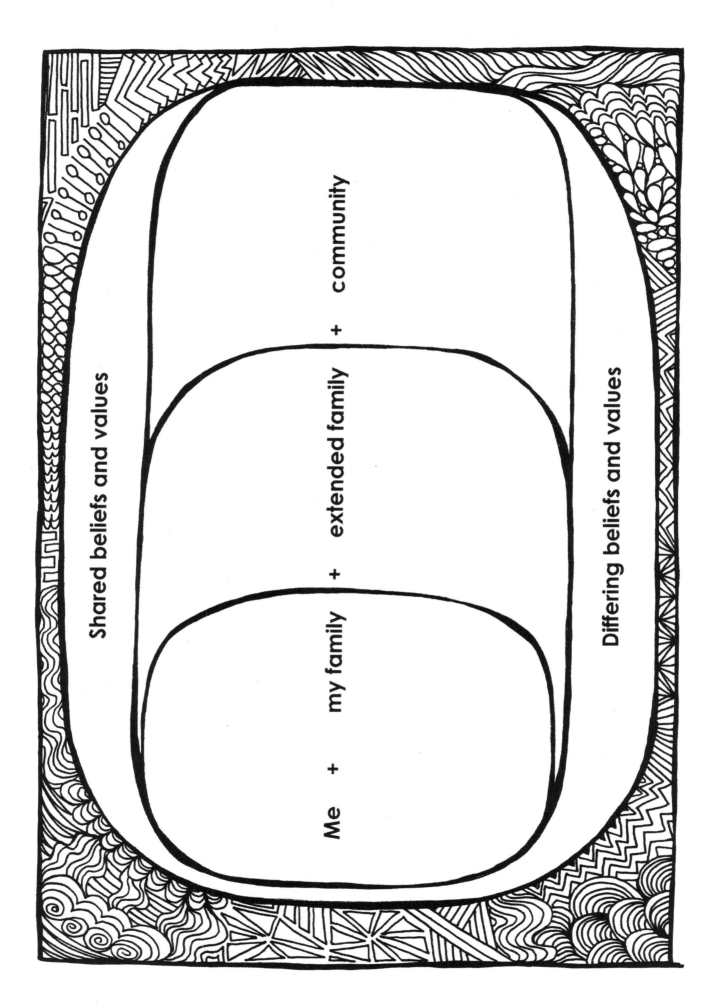

What's the balance of **support or stress** that your extended family brings to your life?

Stress

Support

What's the balance of **support or stress** that your partner's extended family brings to your life?

Stress

Support

If you were to colour-in this picture, as a family, how would you go about this?

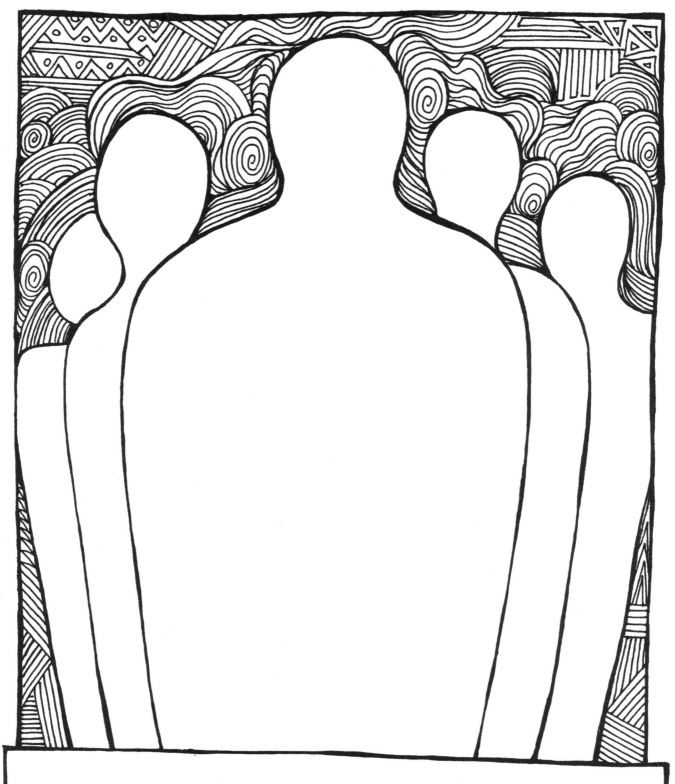

What does it mean to you to be a **member** of your family?

Chapter 4

Communication and Conflict Resolution

Many people seek therapy wanting to learn how to improve communication with others, to reduce conflict between family members and to create more peace within the family. The way we communicate can help us build deep and meaningful bonds with others, whilst allowing us to express ourselves, letting us feel validated and understood. Improved communication in partner relationships helps to build emotional intimacy; distance often develops if communication is a problem. Writing about couples learning communication skills, Hewison *et al.* state: 'Their purpose is to improve the quality of their interactions, so helping them feel more connected and in tune with one another' (2014, p.126).

Many people actively avoid communication if the topics or themes are difficult or painful to discuss. This can result in a cyclical problem of feeling stressed and having heightened emotions which hinder calm and effective communication. Some worksheets aim to explore these in order to enhance the facilitation of therapeutic change.

Theoretical perspectives
Systemic theory

Communication is often considered only in the verbal sense, and yet all behaviour can be seen as communication in the context of others. Within the family system, communication is the essence of interactional patterns and connections between members, and is essentially an exchange of information. Rivett and Street write about how 'these connections are established by the process of information exchange (emotional, cognitive or behavioural), which constitutes communication' (2009, p.7). They continue to describe how all actions can be considered as communications:

In a family it is *impossible not to communicate*: Everything that any one person does provides an opportunity for information exchange within and between family members. As an open human system the family can therefore be considered to be defined by its communicational patterns... Information exchange, what we have termed 'communication' is the fuel of the interaction in human systems. To be human is to communicate and to communicate is to be in relation to someone else. (2009, pp.7, 8)

If all action and activity are seen as communications with others, it is important that the meanings of those activities, along with the contexts that people are in and are influenced by, are understood (Campbell 1994). What is interpreted or 'heard' by the receiver of the information can be far from what was intended by the sender. Much conflict can arise when there are misunderstandings. When writing about relationship therapy, Hewison *et al.* state that when 'couples increase their ability to communicate with each other, more attention can be paid to their implicit as well as explicit feelings, especially when they arise from misconstrued meanings and intentions' (2014, p.136). They add that, 'The hypersensitivity that often accompanies relationship distress increases the likelihood of communications being misinterpreted' (2014, p.137). Many of the worksheets in this chapter focus on exploring our meanings behind what we communicate.

Bateson (1972) developed the idea that communication is a multi-level process, whereby the content of what is being communicated is one level, and the way in which it is communicated is another level. This is described by Carr: 'Each message entails a *metacommunication* about the relationship between the speakers, which is usually conveyed nonverbally' (2012, p.64). Sometimes the communication is contradictory with itself, which is confusing and influential in creating psychological problems within families. Bateson (1972) described this as a 'double bind', where the way a communication is delivered contradicts the content of the communication. Some of the worksheets here aim to clarify people's meanings behind certain behaviours, and help to check out if they are in alignment with the receiver's perceptions.

There are other factors relevant to the quality of communication between people in relationships. Hewison *et al.* write about partners who 'may come from different cultural backgrounds and hold different religious and social beliefs, which may influence what can and cannot be discussed in their relationship... Family scripts and childhood experiences can also define the limits of what can be spoken about' (2014, p.134). Many of the worksheets in this chapter aim to provide platforms for exploration and discussions about the potential constraints to effective communication.

Psychodynamic theory

Communication can be blocked if there are unconscious collusive agreements in place, governing the discussion of certain topics (Hewison *et al.* 2014). These often lead to particular dynamics being played out between people, and is explored in great depth by Eric Berne (1964) in *Games People Play: The Basic Handbook of Transactional Analysis*. Hewison *et al.* state that in couple therapy, it is helpful to support partners to 'express feelings of vulnerability and unmet needs (which may initially be outside awareness) and to understand how anxiety about having these attachment needs met underpins destructive patterns of interaction within the relationship' (2014, p.370).

There are worksheets in this chapter which focus on how we express our emotions, with the aim of exploring if there are any unconscious processes influencing our communication of these.

Cognitive behavioural theory

Facilitating people in learning communication skills makes up a fundamental part of CBT when the focus is about family and couple work. These techniques aim to help people in 'communicating messages clearly, directly and congruently, checking that one has been understood, listening in an empathic manner, paraphrasing messages and checking the accuracy of such paraphrases' (Carr 2012, p.100). Writing about couple work in particular, in relation to the emotional distance and conflict which usually constitutes distress within a relationship, Carr states that using CBT techniques 'involves helping couples challenge destructive attributions, beliefs, assumptions and expectations which contribute to relationship distress and replacing these with more benign alternatives' (2012, p.370).

The aim, therefore, within some of these worksheets is to promote effective communication between family members and partners, in order to enhance emotional intimacy and understanding and to help reduce conflict.

Identifying and mapping interactional patterns:

Family member's actions

My heightened reactions and responses (include the way you feel, what your thoughts are, how you act...)

Ways I can help to
restore calm

Helpful things other
family members
could do or say

How do you **communicate** to others that you're feeling…?

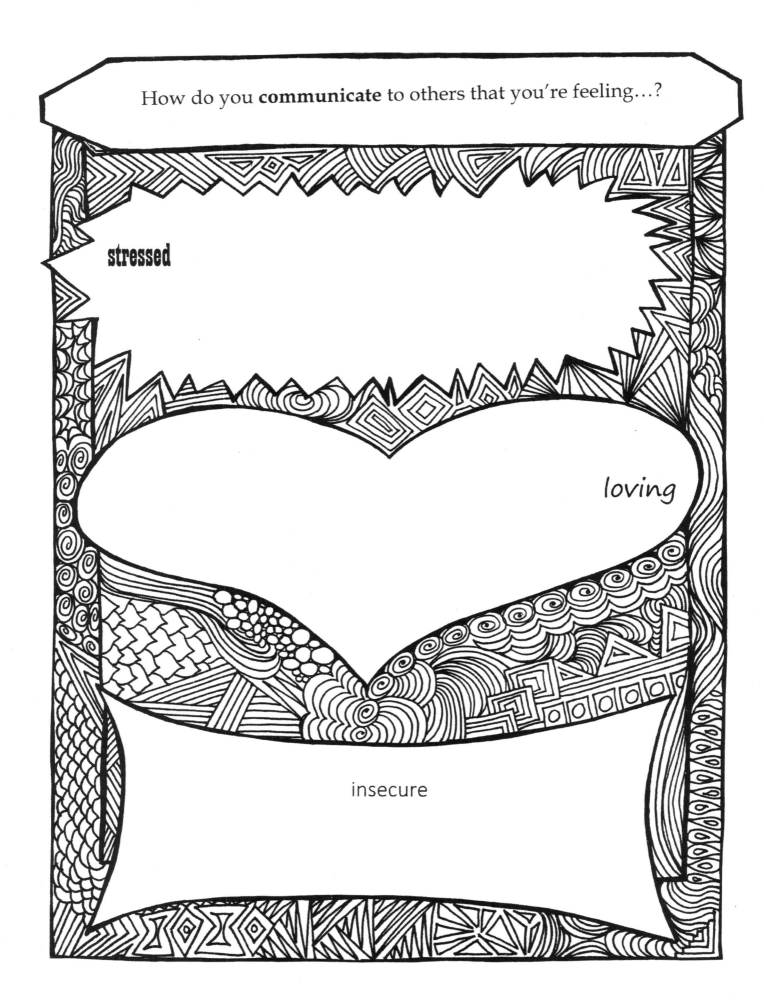

stressed

loving

insecure

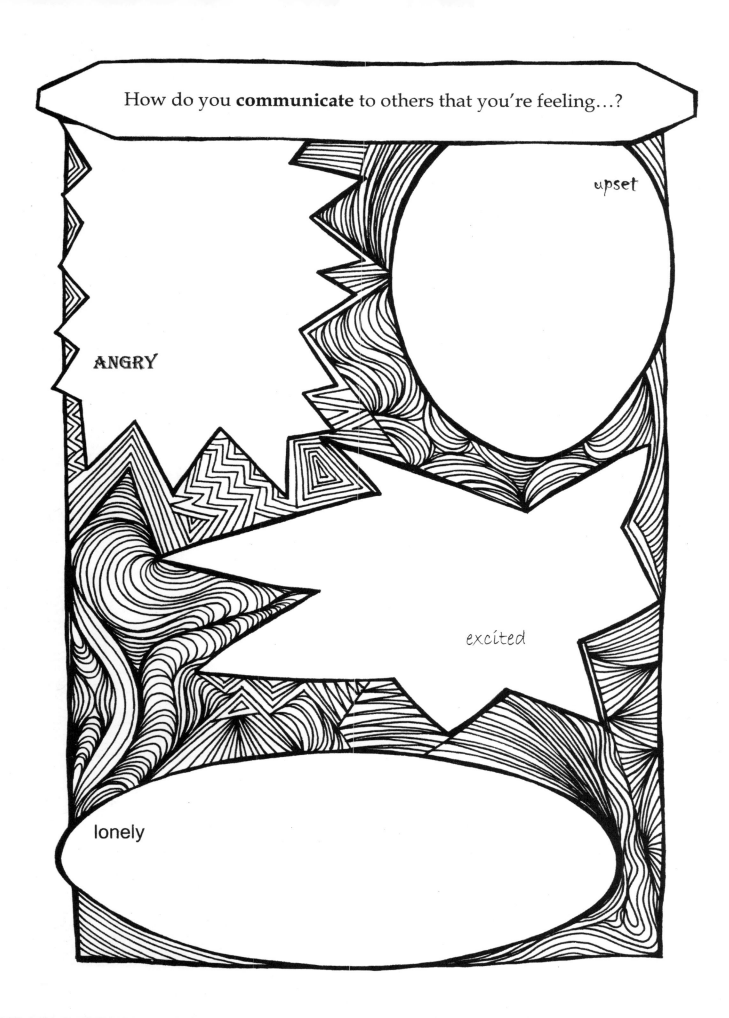

What would show on the front of your t-shirt that you're happy for others to know about you?

What's on the back of your t-shirt that you don't want others to know about you?

For you, which **family rules** are

...absolute?

...negotiable?

You are going to give a speech about yourself: What will you say?

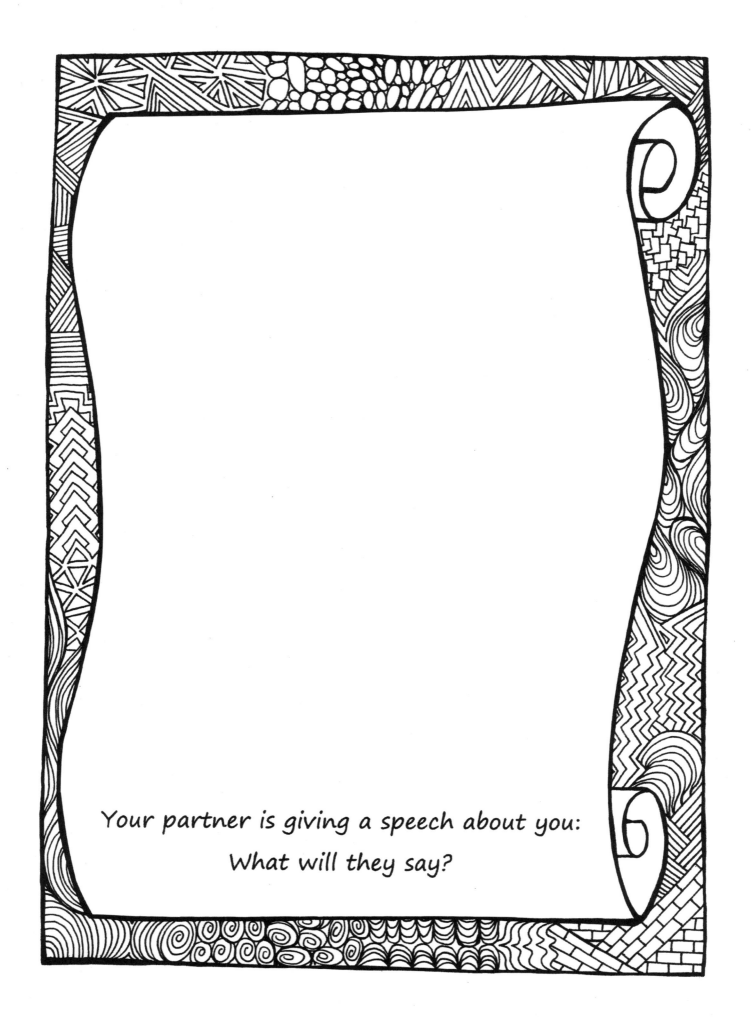

Your partner is giving a speech about you:
What will they say?

Your_____ [family member] is going to give a speech about you: What will they say?

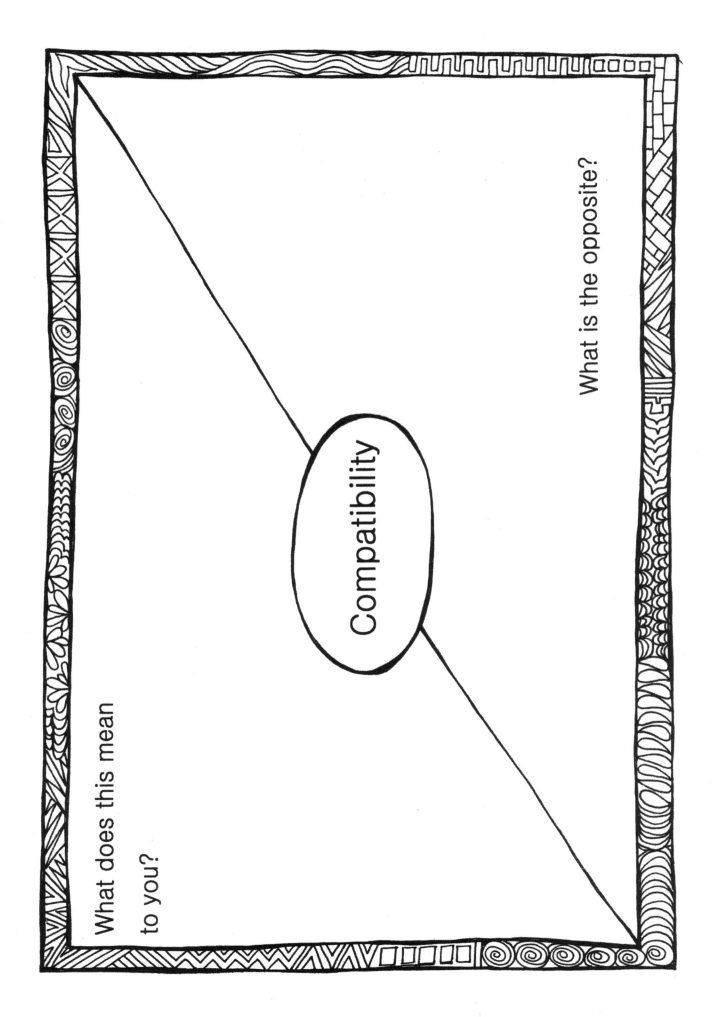

What is the opposite?

Compatibility

What does this mean
to you?

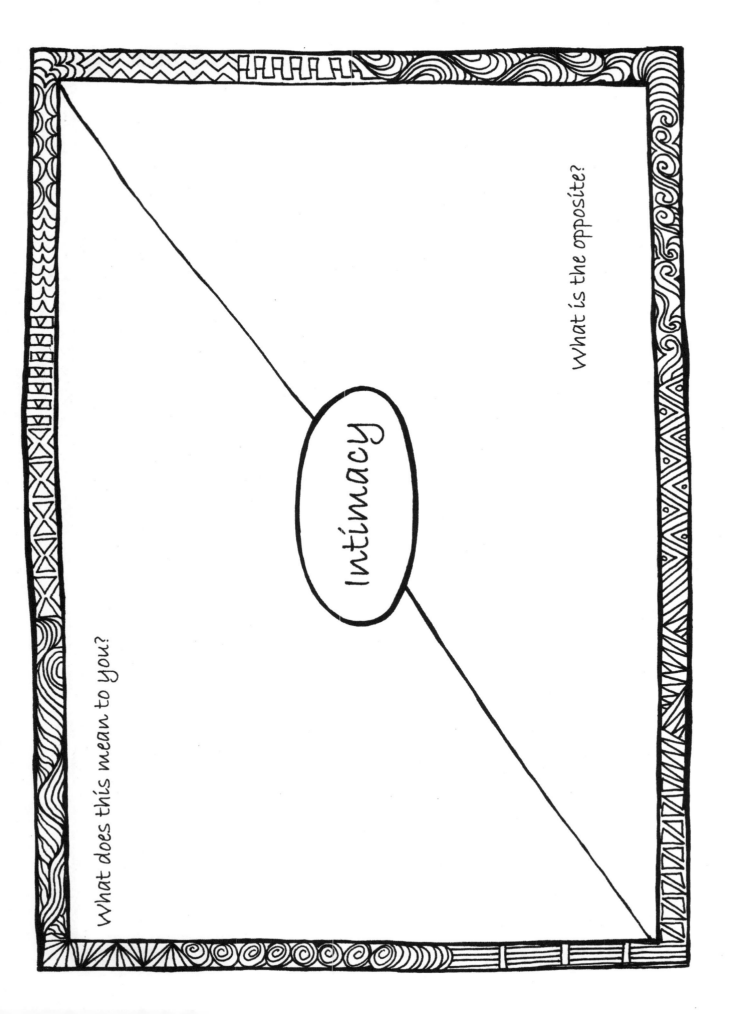

Intimacy

What is the opposite?

What does this mean to you?

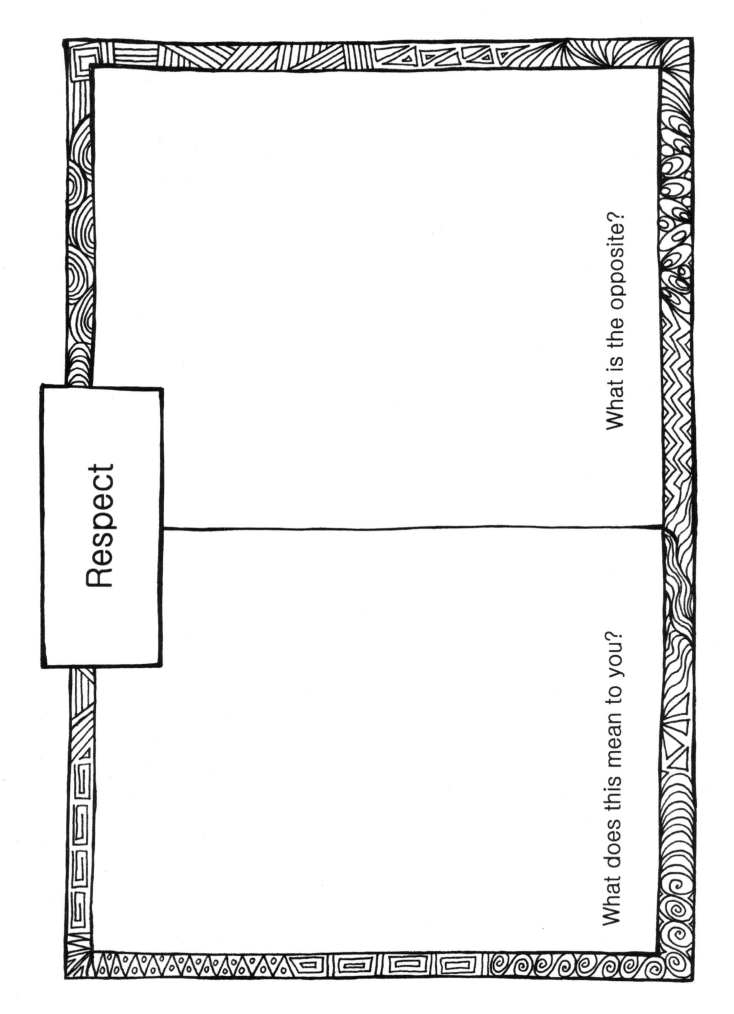

Respect

What is the opposite?

What does this mean to you?

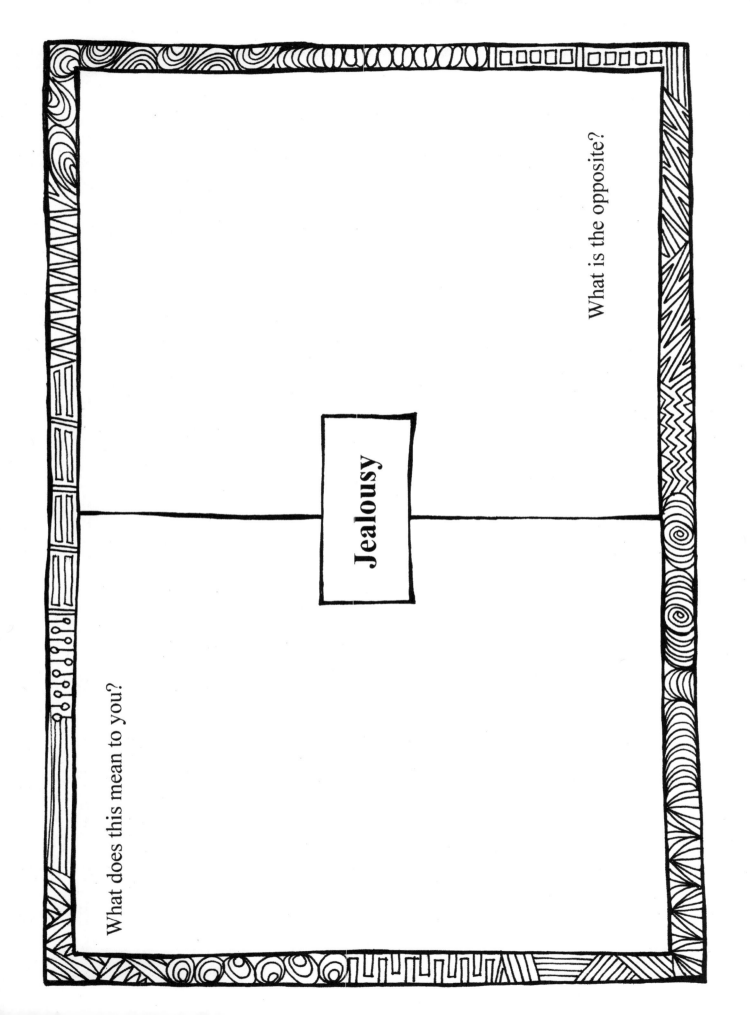

Jealousy

What is the opposite?

What does this mean to you?

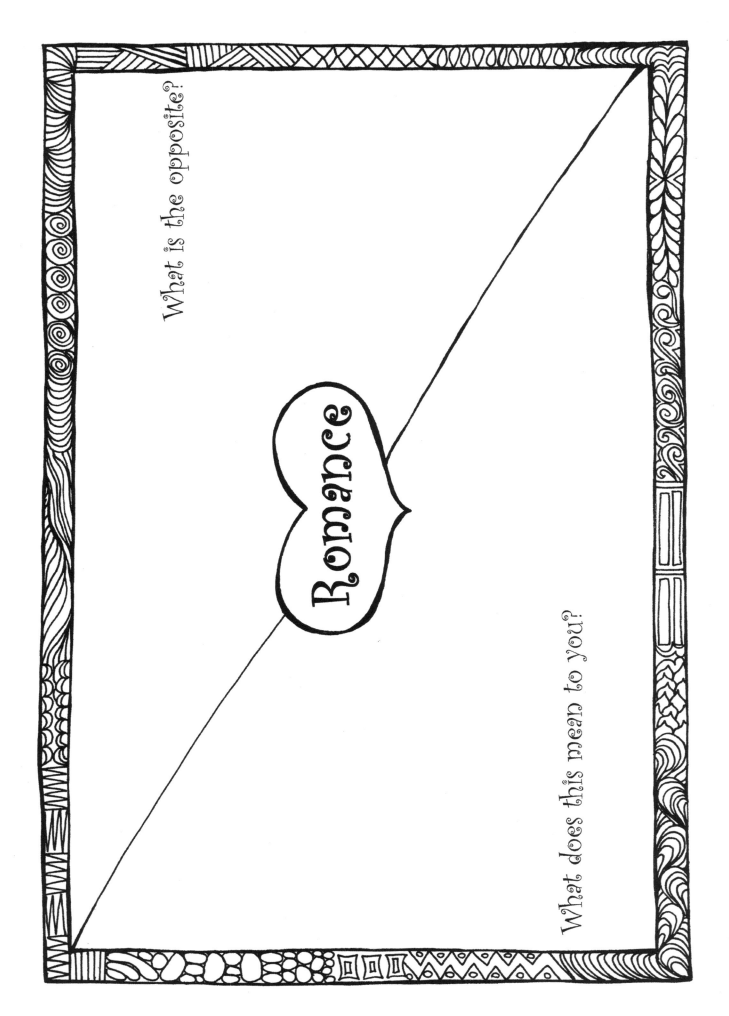

What is the opposite?

Romance

What does this mean to you?

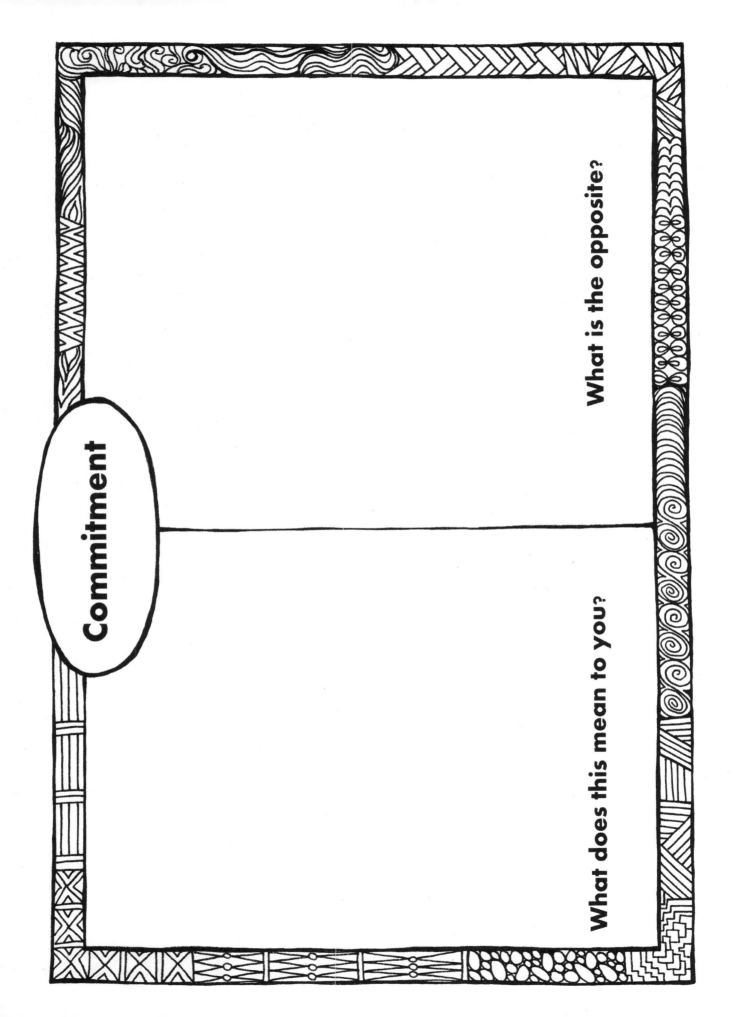

Commitment

What is the opposite?

What does this mean to you?

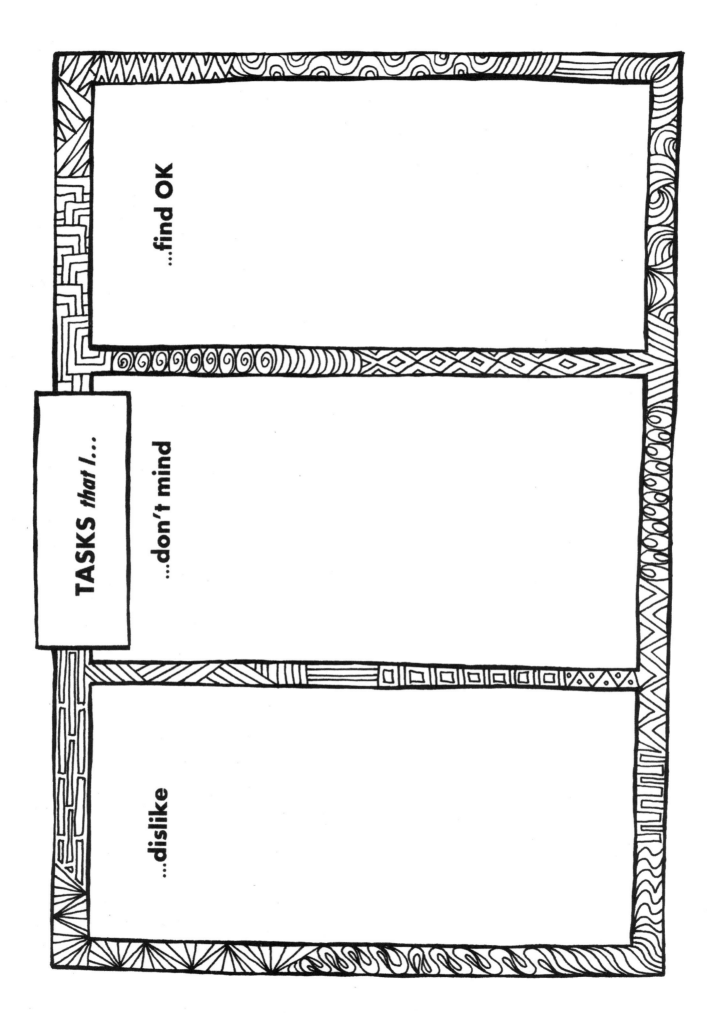

TASKS *that I...*

...find OK

...don't mind

...dislike

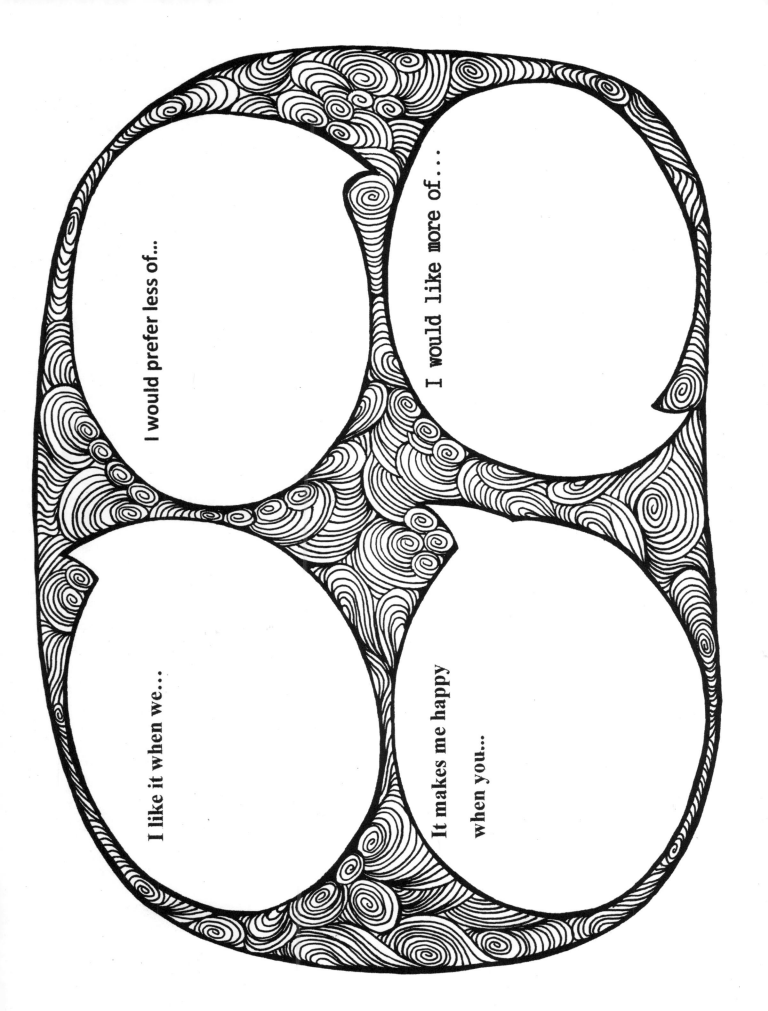

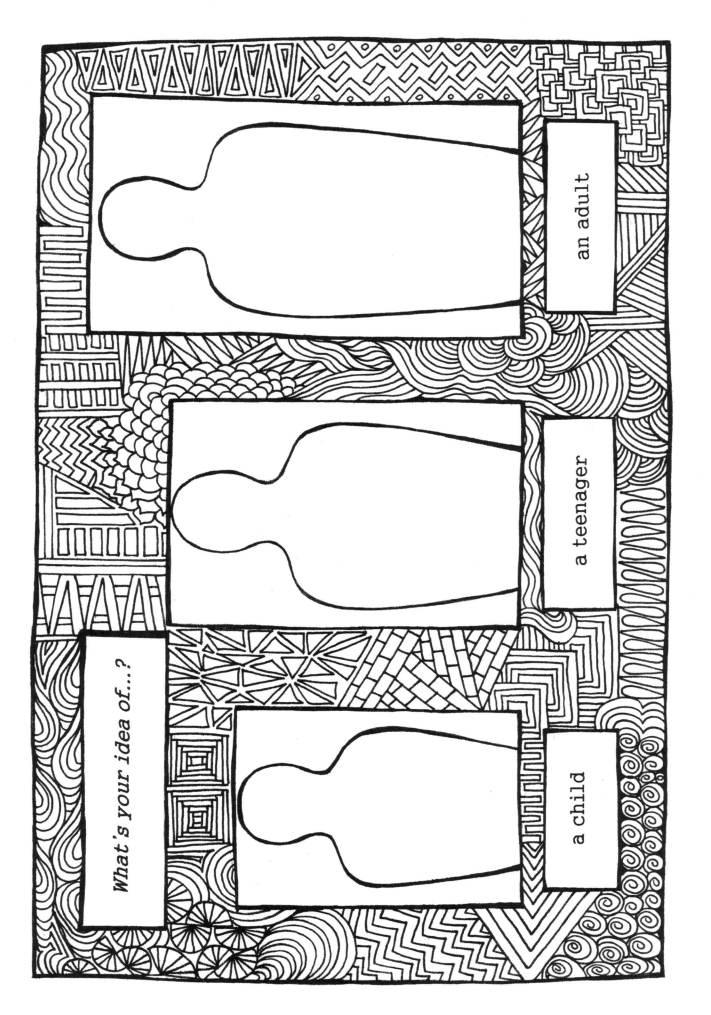

References

Bateson, G. (1972) *Steps to an Ecology of Mind.* London: The University of Chicago Press.

Beck, A., Rush, A. and Shaw, B. (1979) *Cognitive Theory of Depression.* New York, NY: Guilford.

Berne, E. (1964) *Games People Play: The Basic Handbook of Transactional Analysis.* New York, NY: Ballantine.

Campbell, D. (1994) 'Key Systemic Concepts.' In: Campbell, D. *Systemic Work with Organisations,* pp. 9–27. London: Karnac.

Carr, A. (2012) *Family Therapy: Concepts, Process and Practice.* Chichester: J. Wiley & Sons.

Christensen, A. and Jacobson N.S. (2000) *Reconcilable Differences.* New York, NY: Guildford.

Craik, K. (1943) *The Nature of Explanation.* Cambridge: Cambridge University Press.

Hewison, D., Clulow, C. and Drake, H. (2014) *Couple Therapy for Depression: A Clinician's Guide to Integrative Practice.* Oxford: Oxford University Press.

Holmes, J. (1993) *John Bowlby and Attachment Theory.* London: Routledge.

Jacobson, N.S. and Christensen, A. (1996) *Acceptance and Change in Couple Therapy: A Therapist's Guide to Transforming Relationships.* New York, NY: Norton.

McGoldrick, M. (1999) 'Genograms: Mapping Family Systems.' In M. McGoldrick. *Genograms: Assessment and Intervention,* 2nd edition, pp.1–12, New York, NY: Norton.

Rivett, M. and Street, E. (2009) *Family Therapy: 100 Key Points and Techniques.* E. Sussex: Routledge.

White, M. (2007) *Maps of Narrative Practice.* New York, NY: Norton.

White, M. and Epston, D. (1990) *Narrative Means to Therapuetic Ends.* New York: Norton.

Willi, J. (1977) *Couples in Collusion.* New York, NY: Jason Aronson.